"The beauty of Colin's knowledge is that he's been there and done that. He speaks from his own experiences, bringing the real world to the learning circle. So listen, and listen good, you don't want to miss a thing." *Brian Bramble, Clifton Accountants, Bomaderry NSW*

"Quite simply, Colin's influence on Australian business is profound. He helps accountants drive better, more resilient, more profitable business and in turn we help our clients drive better, more resilient, more profitable businesses. His raising of the bar goes well beyond the firms he has direct contact with." *Nathan Williams, Brindleys Chartered Accountants, Mudgee NSW*

"Warning!: This book will give your accounting business an unfair advantage, hide it from your competitors!" *Matthew Snelleksz, Snelleksz & Co, East Brisbane, QLD*

"Colin has been instrumental in guiding and developing our business over the past 12 months. Colin's knowledge in all facets of what makes an accounting business work coupled with his desire to innovative and challenge the status quo is exceptional." *Justin Flavel, Flavel Tierney, Subiaco WA*

"I find Colin totally fabulous - he is an excellent communicator who has inspired me to make grand leaps with the vision for my business. The depth and breadth of his knowledge of the accounting industry is unsurpassed. His style is warm and accessible and should engage any potential readers." *Tracey Amott, Greenview Accounting Group, Bunyip VIC*

"If you want to know how to run an accountancy BUSINESS, not just a practice, ensure you obtain advice from a true expert, one who has been doing it successfully for over twenty years. Colin doesn't theorise or preach, but lets you see how ordinary accountants can create extraordinary businesses. This will be an invaluable reference for practitioners, and deserves a prominent spot in every accountant's library. So, read it, relate to your situation, adapt for your firm, and enjoy the rewards you deserve." *Cameron Finlay, Arnold & Finlay, Southport QLD*

"Colin's knowledge of the accounting industry and how it works makes his insights invaluable to anyone wanting to grow their practice." *Timothy Munro, Change Accountants, Brisbane QLD*

ACCOUNTANTS
The Natural Trusted Advisors

ACCOUNTANTS
The Natural Trusted Advisors

How proactive value-added services can help you live up to your status.

Colin Dunn

© Copyright 2012 Colin Dunn

Published by VIVID Publishing
P.O. Box 948, Fremantle
Western Australia 6959
www.vividpublishing.com.au

National Library of Australia Cataloguing-in-Publication data:
Author: Dunn, Colin.
Title: Accountants, the natural trusted advisors : how proactive
            value-added services can help you live up
            to your status / Colin Dunn.
ISBN: 9781922022097 (pbk.)
Subjects: Accountants--Public relations.
            Accounting--Customer services.
            Accounting firms--Management.
            Communication in accounting.
Dewey Number: 657

No part of this publication may be translated, reproduced, or transmitted in any form or by any means, in whole or in part, electronic or mechanical including photocopying, recording, or by any information storage or retrieval system without prior permission in writing from the copyright owner. Information included in the book 'Accountants: The Natural Trusted Advisors' represent the views and experience of the author. Whilst the examples, concepts and principles have resulted in success and business improvement for many firms, nothing in these pages shall be taken to constitute legal or other professional advice and is provided for your information only. Nixon Advantage and the publisher assume no responsibility for information contained in these pages and disclaims all liability in respect of such information. Details in this book are believed to be correct at the time of writing. The author has researched all sources to ensure the accuracy and completeness of the information contained in this book. However, no responsibility is taken by the author or publisher for any errors, inaccuracies, omissions, or any other inconsistency herein.

This book is dedicated to my wife Wendy and our beautiful children, Matthew and Daisy. You all continue to challenge me to become a better husband and father. The support you give me to allow me to do what I do is unfailing. I love you dearly.

Contents

Chapter 1: Why are you an accountant?   1
    Do you have a job, a career or a vocation?
    Do your clients believe what you believe in?
    You have to believe you can do it before your clients will believe you
    Getting the right business model in place

Chapter 2: Who are your ideal clients?   21
    Rationalising your existing client base
    If you want the right clients, stop accepting the wrong clients
    Client selection process for new clients
    Referral strategy for accountants

Chapter 3: Compliance as a springboard to business improvement   37
    Compliance as a commodity
    How to add value to your core service
    The Annual General Meeting
    Leveraging into new opportunities

Chapter 4: Turning wants into needs   53
    Why 'knee-jerking' is costing you serious money
    It is in your clients' best interests to ignore what they say
    The ultimate question to use every time
    Articulating value so that everyone wins

Chapter 5: Showing clients what is possible in their businesses   69
    The power of language
    The power of numbers
    Enabling clients to discover for themselves
    Strengthening objectives using what-if planning

Chapter 6: The power of planning — 87

Most people spend more time planning their vacation than they do planning their business

Why process trumps content

Why clients find planning so valuable

How to create a powerful action plan with guaranteed additional work for you

Chapter 7: Monitoring and accountability — 103

Accountability as a major key to implementation

Stay close to the numbers

Your role is to provoke, not to be liked

The ultimate in proactivity - real time monitoring

Chapter 8: Involving your team — 119

Learning to let go

Developing your 'A' team

Investing in your people

The higher your fee, the lower your involvement

Chapter 9: Building your brand through world class service — 135

Differentiating through client service

Living by your core values and service standards

Systems to make it happen every time

Powerful feedback systems

Chapter 10: Expanding your footprint into niche markets — 153

Essentials for developing a niche

Becoming a content expert

Developing and qualifying your prospect list

Making it happen with a marketing activity plan

1

Why are you an accountant?

Do you have a job, a career or a vocation?

Why did you choose to become an accountant? It is a question that many accountants find hard to answer. Me? I majored in French and spent a year teaching in France. Much as I had a wonderful year abroad, I quickly decided I did not want to be a teacher. Upon my return home, Dad asked me what I was going to do for a career. I had no idea, but I did know that I was good at mathematics. Dad was a banker and he was being courted by a local accountant called Keith, who was managing partner of a small yet fast-growing accounting firm in Chorley, Lancashire. I called Keith and he offered me two weeks' work experience during the university Christmas holidays. At the end of the two weeks, he kindly offered me a job.

So as I reflect on this, I realise that I fell into accounting. I suspect many accountants did likewise. So let me ask a better question to get a better answer; why did you choose to make accounting your career? Why are you STILL an accountant? Most of the accountants with whom I work seem to want more than number crunching.

So do you have a job, a career or a vocation? Here's my definition:

Job: Short term. Week to week or month to month. No long-term aspirations in your current organisation.

Career: Longer term. You are on a path. You seek progression; more interesting and challenging work and you work on building client relationships.

Vocation: You feel as though you are in the right place. It is your 'calling.' You know deep down that you were made to be an accountant and you love helping your clients.

In the early 1990s around and after the time I qualified as a Chartered Accountant, I was heavily influenced by a partner called Martin. Martin used to get very frustrated with what he called the lack of commerciality of some the managers and accountants in the firm. As I reflect on this, I wonder if this might be one of the elements that can help young accountants transition from job to career (and in some cases, to vocation). I find it hard to believe that any young person ever woke up one morning and stated to the world that they believed they had a calling to become an accountant. It is something that grows on you, but for it to grow and flourish, it needs encouragement, nurturing and skills development. When partners complain to me that their people are hopeless and don't get it, my response is that the fish rots from the head down. What are you doing to develop your people? Martin, to his credit, was extremely good at this. He took me out on client visits, had me work as his assistant on value-added projects such as planning sessions and had the confidence to let go and allow me to step up to do business improvement work with his clients on my own.

Why are you an accountant?

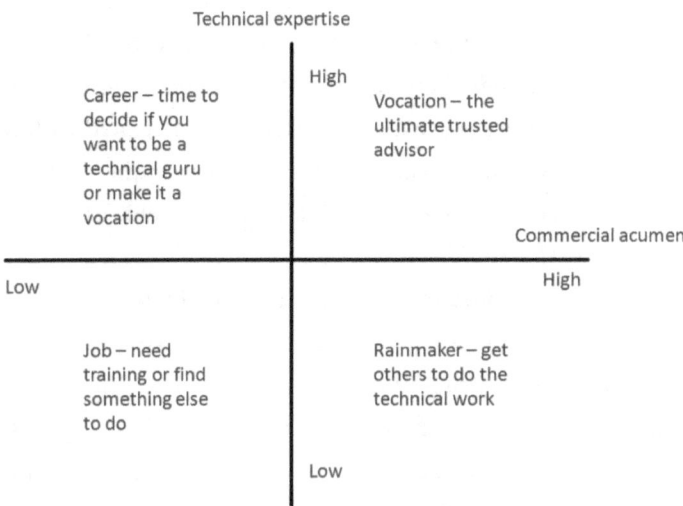

Figure 1.1: What are you doing to move to the top right quadrant?

Earlier this year, I did a couple of straw polls, asking 35 accountants the 'better' question, why are you still an accountant. Here is a summary of the top 10 most common responses:

1. Love working with clients.
2. Meet a variety of people.
3. Get involved in different sorts of work.
4. Contact with interesting people.
5. Fascinated by business.
6. Client contact.
7. Like to see clients succeed.
8. Love to help people.
9. To influence lives.
10. To help clients achieve lifestyles and improve their financial position.

Of course, there were also comments about independence, freedom and the ability to make good money. Most respondents acknowledged these as expected outcomes rather than things that drive and inspire them. Across the three separate groups surveyed, the responses articulated with the most **passion** fell into the ten categories above. And hence the purpose of this book. If it's true that accountants genuinely want to help their clients, then how do you do that?

The accountant is often touted as the trusted advisor to business. And rightly so. But unless you step up and proactively help your clients, that right will be taken away from you. Other professionals such as business coaches, bankers, financial planners and insurance brokers are lining up to step into the trusted advisor role if you vacate it. So given the primary motivators articulated by the accountants I surveyed, I wondered why they were not more proactive. One measure of proactivity would be the number of uncharged nurturing visits made to clients each month. Why are you not doing more, I asked? Specifically, what is stopping you from visiting 20 clients per month to determine what they need and how you can work together to help the client achieve their goals and objectives? Here is what they said:

- Putting out bush fires.
- Chargeable work demands.
- Phone calls/emails.
- Lack of planning.
- Not sure what to say at nurturing meetings.
- Lack of courage.
- We are not sales people.
- Outside our comfort zone.

Frankly, these are excuses, not reasons. When pushed, most of the accountants surveyed conceded that the real reasons could be summarized in one word – fear. Fear of what? There are two big ones:

1. Rejection. Will some clients say no? Of course! Don't worry about it. Some clients will never be interested. All you can do is offer your help. If they choose not to take it, it is not your fault. Our friend Alan Weiss says it beautifully – 'the buyer's job is to buy. If they don't, it's their mistake, not ours.' As long as you like the client and want a long term relationship, wish them good luck, ask if you can check in again in three months time and find another client to go and visit. Your philosophy needs to be to identify opportunities to create massive value for all of your clients then work with those who put their hands up. Imagine if every client said yes – you would never cope with all of the work anyway so don't worry about some saying no!

2. Not knowing the answer. What if a client asks a question to which we cannot respond instantly? This is the curse of the accountant. We are trained to be experts and feel we must be able to answer every question immediately. This is why we go straight to solutions mode all the time. You need to understand that often, your client is better served by you NOT giving them an instant response. And much as it is hard to take, given our technical training and our need to be the expert, 'I don't know' is a perfectly valid response. As long as it is followed by 'I'm going to do some research on that and speak with a couple of the experts in that field at my office (or in my network) then I'll come back to you on Wednesday. There could be two or three ways in which we can do that and I want to make sure we think through all of the options so that you get the best solution.'

Fear is a terrible thing. It suppresses our natural instincts and deprives us (and our clients) of opportunities. So you owe it to yourself to conquer your fears. Well into my late 20's I had a dreadful phobia of public speaking. It was so bad that I was terrified of even contributing in meetings. I was fortunate in that I was mentored by a partner who had gone through a similar experience. He helped enormously. But you make your own luck. Being mentored in and of itself would not have cured the fear. I had to push myself out of my comfort zone and do something about it myself. The turning point for me was attending an external course to help reject that specific fear – every Wednesday evening for 13 weeks. I hated it for the first five weeks but once I became more comfortable I thrived on it and it changed my life.

So if you are in this game to help clients, what to do and how to do it? Before we get there, let's take a step back – and start with what you believe in.

Do your clients believe what you believe in?

Simon Sinek, author of the excellent book, *Start with Why*, is well known for his fastidious assertion that people don't buy what you *do*, they buy *why* you do it. In his TED speech in 2009 (www.ted.com – search on Simon Sinek; the speech is entitled *How great leaders inspire action*) he suggests an important business goal of ultimately only doing business with clients who believe what you believe in. I love that.

So the obvious question is this: what do YOU believe in? Why are you in business? What is your raison d'être? For such a simple question, it is surprisingly difficult to answer.

Keith, the managing partner of the accounting firm I grew up in, was a visionary. He had an uncanny ability to see the bigger picture and to inspire team members and clients to get behind that vision. As a result, the firm attracted quality team members and clients despite its location in a small town in Lancashire. Keith led with the 'why'. He articulated it beautifully like this:

> *Our vision is to help our clients achieve more than they ever thought possible – and to have fun doing it.*

That was our belief. If you didn't believe in that, you were in the wrong place. It took some time to finalize the statement and Keith artfully involved team members in its development. Similarly, I have seen other firms create well thought out and compelling visions or statements of belief. The most important step, however, is to communicate what you believe in to the outside world – specifically, to clients, prospects and key referrers of work. You see, it is impossible for clients to believe in what you believe if you don't tell them what that is!

In our business, we work with accountants to help them offer services in eight key areas:

1. Helping clients grow their business.
2. Helping clients to increase profitability.
3. Helping clients to improve cash flow.
4. Helping clients protect their assets.
5. Helping clients with succession planning and/or business sale.
6. Helping clients with tax minimization.
7. Helping clients financially retire.
8. Helping clients leave a legacy.

It's our belief that these eight services are in the heartland of an accountant's capabilities and that when they are offered consistently to clients, they truly will position the accountant as the trusted advisor. Of course, if you are reading this and you strongly disagree with this philosophy because, for example, you would prefer to churn through 3,000 tax returns in a 'sausage factory' environment, then what we do is not for you.

So let's translate that to your accounting business. If you could wave your magic wand and have your business reflect your beliefs, what would it look like? What would you do? What sort of clients would you work with and how would you interact with them? What services would you provide and how would you deliver them? These are probably the questions going around in your head right now – but you need to resist the temptation to jump to tactics (the how) just yet. All will be revealed in later chapters...assuming you are aligned with our 'why.'

To help you with this important step, try this simple exercise. Reflect on recent times when you have felt really happy with the outcome of your day's work. What happened to fill you with such satisfaction? Was it discovering a $4 difference in a bank reconciliation? Or winning a long battle with the Tax Office that saved a client $7.50? (Don't laugh – there are some accountants whose fires are well and truly lit by such achievements. There is nothing wrong with that – but if this is you, you are not aligned with our beliefs and you may be better off picking up your green pen and getting back to your passion rather than reading the rest of this book!)

If you are still reading, the likelihood is that you answered the question with answers such as these:

- You won a new, high-level client and you can't wait to get stuck into helping them.
- You had some positive feedback from a client as a result of a meeting or other interaction.
- A client called you to tell you of a big win they had.
- You won a large proposal for a value-based project.
- A client turned in monthly or quarterly numbers that overachieved the targets they had set at your last meeting.
- You had a sensational client meeting that left you and your client buzzing.
- You won a big new client as a result of a referral from one of your best clients.
- A non-client or key referrer told you that they heard you have been doing some great work with your clients.
- You generated a new idea that you can turn into IP to use with other clients.
- You ran a seminar with clients and received positive feedback.

If you nodded your head to one or more of the above, then we are getting somewhere with your 'why'. I don't want to put words in your mouth because it is important that you work with your partners and team to articulate what you believe in, but in case you need inspiration, here are some areas to consider to get the juices flowing as you get focused on finding your 'why' (I have heard all of these from accountants):

- We want to help our clients run better businesses.
- We want to do more than just compliance – there is so much more that we could offer.
- We want to be seen as offering real value to our clients.
- We want to make a positive difference in our community.
- We love to see our clients achieve great things.
- We want this to be an exciting place to work.
- Our aim to is quash the stereotype of 'boring accountant' by providing real value.
- We aim to be proactive.

Be careful – all of the above can become motherhood statements if you don't back them up with action. Which is why your next step should be to share what you believe in with your clients. Then go back to Simon Sinek's statement; the goal is to work only with those who believe what you believe in. Over time, your client base should reflect that. (One step at a time; we come to client selection in chapter 2.)

Start with why; what do you believe in? Are you aligned with your partners? Are your team members engaged? How do you best articulate it? Whilst this is not an easy project, I urge you not to over-think it. Once you have something you are reasonably happy with, start talking to your clients about it to gauge their reaction. What's the worst that could happen?

You have to believe you can do it before your clients will believe you

Profits in the accounting profession are far too low. Based on our 2011 survey of accounting firms, only 2.5% of the profession are making over $1 million profit per partner. Most earn much less. For all of the risk assumed in being in business, why bother?

There are many and varied reasons cited as to why such low profitability exists. For example, 'our clients can't afford to pay more', or 'we can't find good people', or 'there is too much compliance work to do, meaning we don't have time to do any high value work with our clients.' Again, most of the reasons cited are merely excuses. It's your business and you choose how you run that business. In my opinion, the major reason why profitability is low is a lack of self-esteem.

The first realization is that you must believe in what you are worth. I believe the profession in Australia has been sent into a negative spiral as a result of the introduction of the GST in 2000. (For international readers, think of the impact of any major tax reform or significant new tax legislation). What was expected to be the golden goose for accountants actually proved quite the opposite, with many firms becoming more and more engaged in low value, transactional, commoditized work for clients. Sadly, the upshot of this has been that client contact has reduced, as has the time available to engage in higher value projects on behalf of clients. This increased focus on low value work for, in many instances, clients with limited potential to enhance the skills of the accountant, inevitably results in accountants feeling that the work they are doing has little, if any, inherent value.

Why are you an accountant?

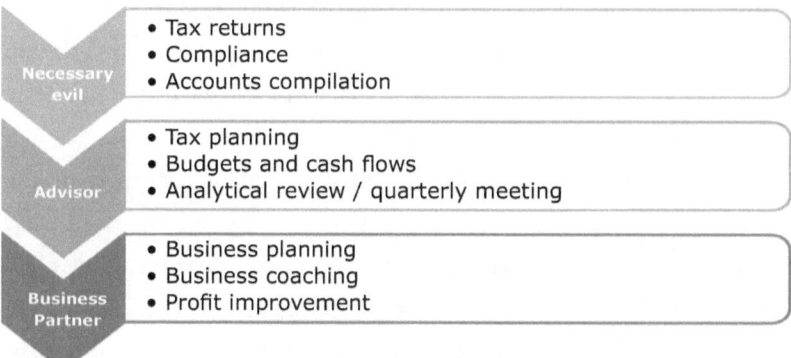

Figure 1.2: What is your current relationship with your clients?

Here is a classic example. Recently I was talking with a partner in a firm that is the only firm in their state to undertake valuation work for a particular industry. They have valuations coming out of their ears, many of them referred from the major banks. They do each valuation at a fixed fee of $2,500. A cursory analysis of their numbers shows that the average hourly rate recovered on these valuations was lower than that for basic tax compliance work. This despite the fact that they are acknowledged experts in the field, they have no competition and every valuation they are asked to do is urgent! I asked when they last increased their prices and the answer was three years ago. My next question was how much have your salaries increased in the past three years – the answer – at least 30% and probably more. It makes no sense.

This particularly affliction is not unique to the accounting profession. I am writing this just prior to Christmas 2011. Recently, my family and I ventured to Sunshine Plaza at Maroochydore, Queensland (Australia) for the annual Christmas shop. It was noticeable that the crowds were thinner than usual. However, what was even more noticeable was every store had massive sales happening. Even the premium department store, Myer, was offering 50% off many lines.

Why would they do this? Two weeks before Christmas; competing against Target and KMart where surely the price sensitive shoppers would go? One would think that people choosing to shop at Myer are not price shoppers. In my view they are throwing money down the drain.

11

How many of your clients are offering discounts to the 90% of customers who never ask for them? As we will discover throughout this book, if you want to lead your clients – and let's face it, many of them need serious advice – you need to sort out your own backyard first.

I recall a social meeting with the then executive chairman of the Australian Wildflowers Association. During our discussion, he asked what I do and I explained that I help accountants improve their businesses. He said he was talking with an accountant just recently who had said there were two things wrong with his business: firstly, he was working too many hours, and secondly, he wasn't making enough money. Wildflower man says to accountant: "That's easy to fix – put your prices up!" Accountant replies: "I couldn't do that, I'd lose clients." Wildflower man makes a seminal insight: "Well, you've just told me you're working too many hours, so why would you worry about losing a few clients?"

Many of the challenges facing the profession have been created by the fixation on using charge-out rates as a basis for billing. This concept is fundamentally flawed for at least two reasons:

1. It makes the assumption that the value to the client is a function of the time taken by you to complete said work AND the charge-out rates that YOU decide upon. In many cases, this is a blatantly incorrect assumption.

2. You are putting a cap on your revenue – and in the booming economy of recent years, increases in expenses (and in particular, salary costs) have outstripped increases in charge-out rates, meaning profits are squeezed further.

So how to change this? It is a leadership issue that starts with the partners or directors making a decision that you are going to build the future growth of your business commensurate with the value you create for your clients, which to my mind is a fundamentally sound proposition. Contrast that to the established view, that growth will be determined by the amount by which we increase our charge-out rates. This makes no sense. How do you look a client in the eye and tell them that the longer you take, the more they pay? Which is essentially what you are saying when you hide behind time-based billing.

Let me give you an example. One of our Proactive Accountants Network members, Stephen, called me to say that his firm had been asked to work on an urgent due diligence project for a client and had quoted $11,000 up front for the work. The client agreed to the fee without hesitation. The accounting firm performed the work efficiently and the job came in at around $6,500 based on charge-out rates. The partner responsible said that he felt guilty billing the $11,000, despite the fact that the client had agreed to the price up front. I asked him the following question: "What if you had set your charge-out rate at $450 instead of $260? Would you still feel guilty?" His answer? "Probably not." And that is the root of the whole problem. Incidentally, there are firms in his city where partners charge out at over $450, which brings us back once again to the self-esteem issue. (There are also many more charging out at less than $260.)

CASE STUDY

Another Stephen, from regional South Australia, really got the concept of unbundling services previously delivered at no charge. Stephen and his team systematically went through each business client's profile so that they had visibility around what each client was receiving from the firm. Having itemized each point of value, the team repriced every single client's work. Interviews were then scheduled with each client to present the new personalized profiles and discuss the changes.

Because of his location in a regional town, Stephen was concerned about losing business hence the reason for the personal interviews rather than sending out a letter to all clients. Shock waves went through the community and Stephen was being approached in the supermarket about the changes in fees. Clients would ring up and say "Stephen's my mate – he wouldn't put the fees up" – but the process was transparent. Stephen smartly told his clients that he was engaged in a business-coaching program so they could understand that he was building a better business and in turn would be able to help them with their own businesses. Since implementing the advice he previously provided for free, Stephen's clients now identify with him for creating a fair and sustainable business.

Rather than losing clients (only four left), Stephen's firm gained 30 new clients within weeks of implementing this process. Of course, the clients shopped around but what they had found was that Stephen's firm was no more expensive than the other firms in the area; they just hadn't been charging for the additional value, so the changes brought the value up to par with the rest of the market.

The entire process took only three months and during client interviews, justification was given on all the work that had been provided for free over the years. This personal approach to up-selling resulted in the firm being able to find an additional $400,000 in revenue that currently wasn't getting charged to clients. As they were already doing the work for each client the revenue from this initiative dropped straight to the bottom line. A salutary lesson in taking a step back and having a good hard look at the value you are providing – are you being fairly rewarded?

So does it matter what sort of services you are providing to your clients? Is there more scope for high prices and higher value if you operate in a niche area or have skills in delivering high-value consulting work to clients? Well, there is certainly more scope for demonstrating value, but no matter what sort of firm you operate, you need to look at yourself and answer a hard question: do you undervalue what you do? Let's take the case of a very small firm where 80% of revenue comes from simple individual tax returns. Upon interviewing the principal of the firm, it transpires that it takes on average 20 minutes to complete such a return and then a fixed fee of $99 is charged. The firm processes approximately 1500 returns each year. Doing the simple maths, this is, on the face of it, a $300 per hour service.

And yet the average hourly rate recovered by this firm is less than $100. How can that be? Upon the principal's own admission, he does over half of the returns himself and feels the need to spend over an hour with each client "chatting with them to build the relationship" – despite the fact that on his further admission, very little additional work is identified and sold as a result of this extra time invested. This is a classic case of over-servicing the client, which happens all the time in this industry. Over-servicing at no additional cost is a by-product of a failure to believe in what you are providing.

What you must do is have more belief in yourself. Here are eight tips to help you do that:

1. Before starting a job, hold a quick brainstorm with members of your team to determine where the value is for the client in the upcoming engagement. Even basic compliance work is more valuable than you think (for example, it can be used for financing, insurance, leasing, business planning, benchmarking, making better management decisions and so on).

2. Communicate more with your clients. Talk with them before and during the work you do for them. Take every opportunity to remind them of the value you bring to the table.

3. Find out what others are charging for the same service. Ask other accountants you know in your locale. DON'T ask 'what's your charge rate?' Ask them specific questions such as 'how much do you charge for a cash flow forecast?'

4. Set prices up front. Be prepared to look clients in the eye and say 'the price is $15,000'. If you have articulated enough value in the project at hand, price will not be an issue.

5. Ask yourself this question: what would happen if you put your prices up by 20% tomorrow? If the answer is 'nothing' or 'not much', bite the bullet and do it.

6. Convince yourself that you are worth more. I am not suggesting motivational seminars and the like; instead, think about the great work you have done for clients over the years and the results your clients have got. Ask clients for testimonials and references. Read them regularly. Most accountants tell me that the majority of their new work comes from referrals – you should have GREAT self-esteem!

7. Get better at asking questions. If the client says I need a cash flow, ask 'why'? The client should then articulate why they perceive the need. No client wants a cash flow forecast just to receive a nice spreadsheet from you. They are likely to tell you that they couldn't pay the wages last week, or the bank is putting pressure on them, or they are thinking of acquiring some new equipment and are not sure if they can afford it, or whatever else is on their mind. Whatever response you get, the likelihood is you will be able to make the client understand what they NEED, rather than what they thought they wanted, and this is where you add value.

8. Sell outcomes, not activities. A firm I interviewed recently had an opportunity to propose for some work to help a client improve their business. The partner's instinctive approach was to print out a business plan template to show the client. As soon as you do that, you are selling a commodity and unless you have a strong relationship, the client might shop your business plan around to try to find a cheaper one. Instead, ask questions to determine the

client's objectives framed as business outcomes, measures and value to the client. When you do that, you will have the confidence to charge more AND your fee becomes academic.

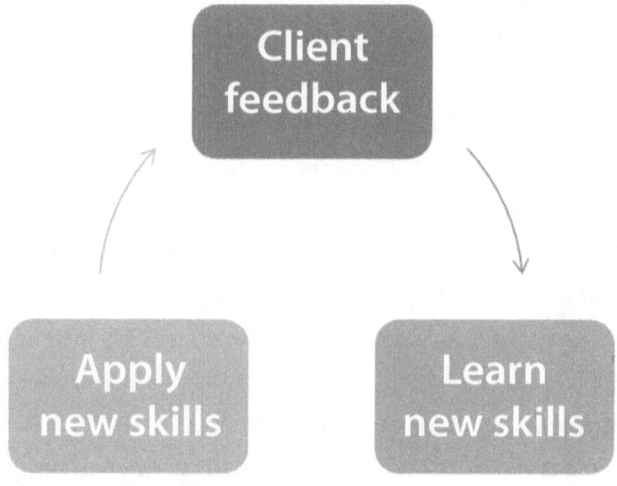

Figure 1.3: Create a positive feedback loop

Let's get rid of this self-esteem issue. Accountants do GREAT work for clients on a daily basis. Remind yourself of the impact you have. Open the lines of communication and talk more frequently with your clients to understand where they perceive value in their interactions with you. And use the confidence you take from that to start earning what you're really worth.

Getting the right business model in place

Most accountants are trained to be technically excellent. There is very little formal training in how to run a successful business. I have even had accountants tell me that they were rebuffed by clients when offering business improvement advice with the line 'what would you know about running a business?' And yet, what do you do every single day? Of course, you are running a business.

The challenge is to set your business up in such a way that it provides excellent cash flow, very high profitability, strong growth combined with the lifestyle you desire. Sadly, many accountants struggle here because they do not have the right business model in place.

If you are driven to make business improvement services a significant part of your firm's revenue, you need to think about the best structure to enable that. In our 2011 Accountants Benchmark Report, we found that the median number of team members per partner in accounting firms was four accountants plus one admin per partner. This supports what I observe on a day-to-day basis. Leverage (people per partner) is a major challenge for accountants. Just recently I was asked by a partner in a high performing accounting firm why I thought that was the case. My response? I think accountants look at the cost of hiring great people before looking at what they would get as a result of surrounding themselves with the 'A' team. As it happened, in a group of 16 accounting firms, the partner asking the question had the highest profit per partner in the room (around $800,000) and the highest leverage (9 people per partner.) He has combined this with low partner productivity – around 27% - to achieve a super outcome.

So what works if your focus is business improvement as a significant offering? Let's take a look at each potential model in turn:

- **Solo.** You are on your own. You have no people. Almost certainly you will be working from home. This is the lone wolf, solo consultant model. You are essentially a consultant, not an accountant. Your major focus is on winning and delivering new projects from your clients. Almost certainly you should outsource your compliance work, as your time is much more valuable identifying high-value projects with your clients. It is rare to see accountants making serious money under this model if they choose to hold onto compliance work.

- **Boutique.** You run a small firm with a niche service, offering business improvement. Your client base should be small and carefully selected (see more on client selection later in this book.) You have a small team around you to look after the compliance side of the business and deliver the 'grunt' work in the business improvement projects that you sell. You might have just 2 or 3 people per partner under this model. As a partner, your focus is on selling and high value delivery.

- **Typical model.** 4 or 5 people per partner. This is where many readers of this book will start from, given this is the median position for accounting firms. Your existing focus will be on tax, accounting and compliance work, which you use as a springboard to identify business improvement projects. Your biggest challenge will be that everyone is too busy dealing with a high volume of compliance. Also, if you are a 'typical' partner, you will be doing a lot of administrative work in the firm, which can have a deleterious effect on your ability to be out with your clients. Your team might even complain that if you brought back more work, it would never get done! If this is you, you need to make a decision – either go back to model 2 or up to model 4.

- **Growth firm.** You invest in the right people to free-up time to enable the partners to be focused on just three things – high value delivery, identifying and selling new projects, and leadership/strategy implementation to drive the firm forward. This means you may need:
    » A professional business manager.
    » A team of client service coordinators to do the administration involved in processing the compliance work.
    » A team of strong accountants.
    » A client manager running each team.
    » A full-time marketing coordinator.
    » Possibly a sales team outside of the partners to find and sell new projects.

If your 'why' involves helping clients improve their businesses, the way you set up your own business is of paramount importance. There is no wrong or right answer – except you should avoid model 3! Here are a couple of examples:

Model 2 – boutique. I met Evan in 2008. He was a frustrated accountant. He was smack in the middle of model 3 and tearing his hair out. He knew that his passion and his natural skill set both lent themselves to high-value work with clients, yet his legacy accounting firm structure was holding him back. After three years of hard work and many ups and downs, he settled on model 2. The firm is now Evan plus 1.5 team members. He has just 20 clients who this financial year will happily pay him an average of $65,000 each. Evan will make $1 million in profit and is loving his work and his 9 to 5 lifestyle.

Model 4 – growth firm. This is the firm I joined in 1987. Growing at 25-30% per annum for the 9 years I was with them was no accident. There was a sales culture in the firm and a heavy investment each year in quality people, including a graduate program and a targeted approach to bring in new people at a high level, both as new, speciality partners and experienced client managers. These people complimented the excellent team members who worked their way through the ranks to senior positions. There was a serious investment in training and development and constant marketing and product development to ensure all clients' needs were met. The firm ended up being an early acquisition of a leading consolidator of accounting firms in the UK. The investment and client focus made it a very attractive proposition for that buyer.

Your challenge is to determine where you are today and which model suits your personality, style and aspirations best. The decisions you make today should reflect the business you are designing for the future. Understanding why you do what you do and articulating that in a way that makes sense to your ideal clients will propel you forward. And it is ideal clients to whom we turn in Chapter 2.

2

Who are your ideal clients?

Rationalising your existing client base

If you are like most accountants, your client base will be a farrago of clients perfectly suited to your firm, mediocre 'we can live with them' types and, sadly, clients where the very mention of their name creates a knot in your stomach. At almost every speech I give to accountants, I ask, 'who in the room has at least one client that you do not like?' Almost without exception, every hand goes up. (The only time this year not every hand went up was when Evan from the previous chapter was in the room. He is delighted with his 20 clients.) Why do we live with this? Remember, it is your business, you make the rules and one major rule should be rationalizing your client base so that it fits with your beliefs (back to the why) and your proposed service offerings. Remember Simon Sinek – the goal is to work only with those who believe what you believe in.

When I suggest client classification as a project, it is often warmly embraced by accountants. I think that is because they envisage a spreadsheet with categories and weightings...happy days for many accountants! Joking aside, if you are going to categorize your clients, think first about the reason why you would do that. Here are three reasons to consider:

1. To determine who your 'A' class clients are and then design a communication schedule for those clients (which you should communicate to them)! Your ultimate goal should be to only work with 'A' class clients.

2. To prioritise the order in which you visit your clients to identify opportunities to help them. 'A's first, then 'B's and so on.

3. To determine once and for all those 'D' class clients (or below) so that you can remove them from your client list. I am regularly told that there is nothing so empowering as firing a 'D' class client. One of our members, Rob, in regional Western Australia, swears by his annual client cull – and this in a town of 3,000 people.

To help you with this process, I have designed a set of client selection criteria specifically for a firm focused on business improvement work with clients. Feel free to choose criteria from the list that resonate with you; equally, you may add your own and ignore any of my suggestions that are not important to you. The key is to pull together a tight group of criteria that feel right to you and your team. This is more art than science. Here are my offerings:

- **Decent fee**. Experience shows that a client that has previously made a decent investment with you is more likely to increase his investment with you in the future. By 'decent' I mean they are used to investing, say, $10,000 plus with you each year.

- **Affordability – revenue >$1M with good profit margins.** Business improvement work done properly doesn't come cheap. As such, you should prioritize clients with the ability to pay you for the value they will receive from your services.

- **Scope for improvement.** If you look at a business and can see opportunities for making a difference, give this one a tick. The place to start is with their management reporting systems. I can tell you without fear of contradiction that once you help a client identify the key drivers of revenue and profit in their business and then engineer systems to extract that data so that it can be monitored and acted upon in a timely manner, the numbers will start to improve almost as if by magic. There will come a time when that improvement will dwindle and you need to step in and take action to drive them to the next level but scope for improvement in management reporting systems is a big opportunity waiting for your expertise to unlock it.

- **Desire to improve.** It's all very well you identify how you might help a client but they need to want it as well. Clients who are enthusiastic and open to collaboration to improve their business trump those who are apathetic and happy with their lot.

- **Takes advice.** I would work with a client who has a track record of implementing my advice any day over one whom my business partner, Rob Nixon, might call NATO – No Action, Talk Only. Think back to previous meetings with the client. When you offered advice, what happened as a result of it?

- **Positive mindset.** Is the glass half full or half empty?

- **Referrer or potential to refer in future.** So much new work for accountants comes from client referrals that it makes sense to prioritize those with a track record of sending new clients your way. Do not exclude a client who has not yet referred, however; it may be your fault if you have never asked.

- **Good payer.** The last thing you want is to find your mental energy absorbed with debt recovery when you should be 100% focused on helping the client achieve their goals.

- **Case study / testimonial.** Put simply, you should have one from every single A class client. Front and centre on your website. Utilize video testimonials for even more dramatic effect. Call your top 10 clients (based on gut feel) and ask them if they would mind you writing a case study about the work you have done together or providing you with a written testimonial for use in your marketing. A class clients will not refuse.

- **Well known in community.** Especially if you are in a remote or regional location. Clients who are well connected can be heavily influential in you winning quality new work.

- **Supports your events.** If you put on a seminar, who are the clients who turn up consistently to support you?

- **You like them.** Let's face it. For all of us on this planet, time is a scarce resource. You only have a certain number of working hours left in your life. Don't waste it with idiots. I recently attended a workshop run by Alan Weiss. In the pre-work for the workshop, Alan asked a truly great question: how much of the time can you genuinely tell me you are having fun?

- **Your team likes them.** Not to be overlooked. Sometimes a client will be nice as pie with you then act like a Rottweiler with your team. This needs to be addressed otherwise your team will lose faith in your client classification policy.

I love this approach to client classification from one of our Proactive Accountants Network members, Matthew in Brisbane:

> "I find the A, B, C rating very boring and prefer something visual or that I can picture in my mind. I came up yesterday with the concept of My Universe, that is, who I want in it and who I want to be surrounded by. It is an interesting view but it works for me and is totally original:

- Stars – these are the brightest heavenly bodies and I want to look at them all day long. My most important clients. They are bright and are stellar performers, the best clients.

- Black holes – clients who suck the life out of you. Get rid of them and stay far away from them. They want everything and pay for nothing. They reflect nothing and absorb all your time.

- Moons – natural satellites. They orbit you and you want them around you because they reflect light to you like our moon. These are clients and referrers who are not stars but reflect stars to you. Keep them and encourage them to continue to refer quality clients to you.

- Asteroids – small bodies, usually cold ice-like rock. There are thousands of them floating around like space junk. These are the smaller clients, the individual tax return clients. A dime a dozen. Avoid them.

- Meteors – they pass through your universe once a year. These are your once a year compliance clients. You want them to be Stars so you can see them more often so try and convert them with more regular projects.

> *"Surround yourself with stars, not black holes or space junk."*
> *Matthew of Brisbane*

If you want the right clients, stop accepting the wrong clients

Irrespective of how much potential still exists within your existing client base, it's my firm belief that every firm needs new clients. The law of entropy suggests that it is impossible to stand still and make progress; every plateau on which you stand will ultimately erode. So just to stand still, we need to be moving forward. This alone should compel you to get very focused on your branding, positioning and lead generation activities.

Here are ten other reasons why new clients are important:

1. New clients create energy. They inject a certain vibrancy into your organization. A regular inflow of quality new clients brings with it a 'feel good' factor. Good people want to work in growing, successful businesses and new clients being introduced to the firm is a great KPI by which team members subconsciously measure the success of a firm.

2. They provide you with a reason to celebrate. In our business, we have a bell on the wall in the main office. The bell is rung every time a new firm joins the Proactive Accountants Network. When the bell rings, everyone cheers and there is a real buzz around the place. People want to know who the new member is and a little bit about them. The person who introduced the new member is congratulated publicly. And since the number of members we serve is a critical number in our strategic plan, every bell is a clear indicator that we are making progress towards our goals.

3. New clients (of the right type) bring with them new challenges and new demands. Most people change accountants because they want better service and more services. So you will often find that new clients demand help from your firm over and above tax and accounting. This in and of itself forces you to learn and implement new skills. And of course, you should be proactively looking for those opportunities rather than waiting for the client to call.

4. New clients require new ideas. With the same old clients year after year you can get stale. An injection of new blood can impel you and your team to do some serious thinking about ideas that you can take to the new client to delight them and help them overachieve their goals. A peripheral benefit is that you can then take those ideas and brainstorm with your team which other clients they might be relevant for.

5. Client service lifts. It's funny how team members lift their game when communicating with new clients. This is inherently wrong but it seems to me that new clients benefit from your 'A' game whereas with existing clients things can be somewhat blasé. So capture the service ideas that come out of working with new clients, continually raise the bar, then formalise your ideas as performance standards to be rolled out to the ENTIRE client base.

6. A new client is an opportunity for another new client. New clients open up a new pot of referral potential. When you take on a new client you should pre-frame for them that in six months' time, and assuming they are delighted with what you have done, you will be asking them for the names of two business owners who would benefit from your service and services.

7. A new angle on testimonials. I sincerely hope you have many testimonials from your existing clients talking about how they have benefited from working with your firm. What about asking new clients for a testimonial outlining why they chose to become a client of your firm? If they have chosen you, there is a reason. Capture it and leverage it in your marketing.

8. Every new client is an opportunity to upgrade your client base. You should only be taking on new clients of the type you want to have – 'A' class clients or, at the very least, clients who have the potential to quickly become 'A' class clients. In most cases, if you follow this mantra, the quality of your client base will be incrementally improved every time

you take on a new client. You can take this one step further by adopting this supplementary strategy: every time you take on a new business client, weed out two or three clients that you know you should not be serving.

9. New clients have no baggage. You have an opportunity to introduce new approaches without worry about what the client might say. I hear all the time that it is much easier to introduce upfront pricing and payment upfront with new clients (although I have to say that is often an excuse for not doing it with existing clients)! But seriously, with new clients you can change the rules. Like establishing the ways in which people can QUALIFY to be a client of your firm. Or even establishing a waiting list to become a client.

10. Set a minimum service standard. With all new clients, I believe you should be doing an annual planning session as a matter of course; you should be seeing them face to face at least four times a year; holding an AGM with them; have a live budget and cash flow forecast; be monitoring their numbers on a monthly basis. With new clients, you set the rules (and then transition those rules to existing clients gradually). If potential new clients turn around and say 'I don't want that, I just want a cheap tax return' then have the business card of your closest competitor at the ready. Let them clog up their book, leaving you to find even more ways of creating value for your clients.

You see, every time you take on the WRONG sort of client you are wasting your own and your team's time and energy. Most accountants tend to take on all comers. You will find that when you start turning clients away, you will become very focused on finding the RIGHT sort of client to grow your firm.

CASE STUDY

A firm I worked with in the United Kingdom found that because of its location, it attracted a lot of passing traffic, predominantly from subcontractors. At the time, the firm's offices looked and felt like a typical accountants' office. They decided to splash out on a lavish decoration project for their reception area. Once the project was completed, anyone walking in would immediately have the impression that they had just entered the most expensive accounting firm in the town. True to form, the price sensitive subbies turned on their heels and went looking elsewhere!

Client selection process for new clients

So how do you stop taking the wrong sort of client? It's all in the language (both the words you say and the chatter going on in your head.) Whenever you have an initial meeting with a prospective client, your mindset needs to be that you are evaluating this prospect to ensure that they are the right client for you. Stop feeling under pressure to sell yourself to the prospect. It should be exactly the other way around – what do they have to do to become a client of your firm?

Figure 2.1 outlines my recommended approach to qualify the prospect. Before you move to determine needs and certainly well before any discussion on price, it is important to establish that the prospective client understands your approach to working with your clients (as a business partner, focused on helping them achieve their objectives, for example). You should also ascertain how they came to hear of your firm and what they know of you. If they were referred by one of your best business improvement clients, you know right away that this is potentially a good fit.

You will know in the first 15 minutes or so if the client is a good fit for you as long as you follow this sort of approach and use language that places you in control. Sense check the personal chemistry. Are you enjoying the discussion or is it hard work? And very importantly, watch out for red flags such as, 'how much is this going to cost me.' A client that comes to you on price will almost certainly leave you on price. You need to be firm in rebutting such a question by responding, 'I don't know yet. Let's get focused on what you need.'

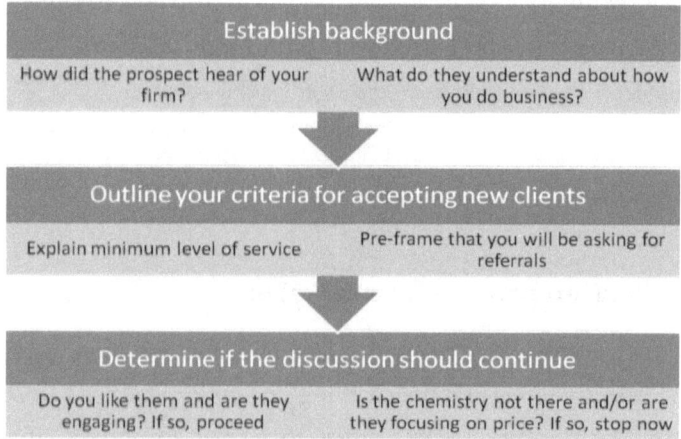

Figure 2.1: Qualifying your prospect – who is in control, you or the prospect?

Once again, come back to your 'why'. My friend John runs a very successful accounting business north of London in the UK. His client selection criteria are simple: he tells prospects that what he does is help his mates make millions. The simplicity of this approach is elegant. If there is no personal chemistry and/or the prospect is focused on price rather than value creation, it is not a good fit and John would be wasting both his and the prospect's time by continuing to dance around trying to sell himself.

Here is your step-by-step approach to attracting new clients of the type you want:

1. Nurture your existing 'A' class clients. Establish and **implement** a client communication schedule with them. Use the following template as a framework to develop your own communication schedule:

    - We will hold an Annual General Meeting with you after the completion of your annual accounts. The focus will be on explaining the numbers and planning for the year ahead. We will present your numbers to you in a graphical manner, explaining critical data such as where your cash went and the key drivers of revenue and profit.

    - We will hold three additional face-to-face meetings with you during the year at your premises. These are 'touch base' meetings to discuss how your business is travelling and an opportunity to bounce ideas off me.

    - We will prepare interim accounts for you in the final quarter of the financial year to enable effective tax planning.

    - We will hold a tax-planning meeting with you once your interims are prepared.

    - You have ad hoc access directly to me by phone and email at any time during the year.

    - You will receive our monthly newsletter, the focus of which is on business growth strategies.

    - We will invite you to connect with us via our social media sites on LinkedIn, Twitter, Facebook and our blog. We distribute relevant and timely sound bites of value to our clients through these means.

- You will receive two free tickets to our seminars and events.
- Once you have worked with us for three months, and assuming both parties agree it is appropriate, we will invite you to join our inner circle of premium clients so that you can share ideas with non-competing business owners.
- We will undertake an annual business assessment and prepare a report measuring your progress year on year.
- We will undertake an annual analysis of profit improvement potential for your business.

2. Implement a proactive referral strategy. See the next section of this chapter for details on how to do this.

3. Create case studies of the great work you have done with clients. Include photos of you with the client, video and written testimonials and display them prominently in your reception area, on your website and in all of your marketing materials.

4. Do great work with clients and ensure others know about it.

5. Develop your skills so that you can confidently move into new areas. Invest in external training or coaching. Acquire best practice products as enabling tools to help you achieve results with clients.

6. Once again, to reinforce what I believe is the most important point; stop taking on all comers. Hold a stock of your competitors' business cards and refer bad fits on to them.

Referral strategy for accountants

Referrals are the lifeblood of a thriving accounting business. They are low-cost pre-qualified leads, which with a bit of work on your end, can be converted into excellent clients very quickly. There are several ways in which you can ask clients for referrals. Whichever you choose, please do it only with your best clients – your 'D' class clients have friends just like them! Here is a selection of ideas:

- **By letter.** Figure 2.2 provides an example letter that you might consider sending to your 'A' class clients to attract more like them.

- **In the language you use.** When you go out to see them, they will invariably ask 'how is business?' Every time you reply 'we're flat out' you are killing referrals dead right there and then. No one wants to refer work to a key advisor who is flat out. Try instead 'business is great and we are always looking for more. Specifically, we're looking for more clients like you who would benefit from our services. Do you know anyone I should be talking with?' You can also use joint accountability statements when embarking on any projects, pre-framing for the client that assuming they are delighted three months into the project, you will be asking them for the names of two contacts who would benefit from a similar approach to helping them. And then follow through and ask.

- **Simply asking, face to face.** Perhaps the most effective mechanism. Figure 2.3 contains a script. Feel free to use or adapt it.

- **Whenever you get a new lead, find out immediately where it came from.** If it is from a referral, thank the client or introducer with a personal phone call. Then, when the new client is on board, apprise them of that fact and thank them again. Or, if it didn't work out, let them know that too, taking the opportunity to re-educate the client where necessary on your ideal client requirements.

- **Create a great experience that clients can talk about.** What do clients think/see/feel when they enter your office? Put your client eyes on and try it for yourself. What is it about your office that makes it stand out from others? If there is nothing, what a great opportunity to change that – quickly. In the firm I worked with in the UK, we had a steady stream of referrals sent by bankers who told their customers 'you need to go and check out this accounting firm; it just feels like a great place.' When you walked into reception, the smell of fresh coffee and the original art on the wall left an immediate impression. Combine this with case studies displayed in your reception area and a fastidious attention to detail and performance standards and you are one large step on the road to receiving referrals of the type you want.

- **Look and act as though you are successful.** Drive a nice car and don't be afraid to park it outside your client's office. I hear too often from accountants that they are scared of buying a prestige car for want of looking TOO successful. Crazy thinking. Dress well. Look the part. People want to deal with professionals who are successful. One of the worst traits I see in accountants is sloppy dress standards. If you want quality referrals, put on a quality act.

Figure 2.2 Sample letter to send to 'A' class clients asking for referrals:

Dear <FirstName>,

We have worked together for quite some time and I would like to think that you are very happy with our service.

I would like to extend my services to assist your professional colleagues in the same way I help you. It is important that you know I am only asking a select group of my clients for this consideration; clients whom I like and for whom I provide a premium level of services.

I would be very grateful if you would please let me know who else in your professional network might benefit from a discussion with me.

To help you with this, please find enclosed a number of my business cards should you find yourself in a position to be able to pass some of these on.

Please call me on [number] should you wish to discuss this initiative with me.

Figure 2.3 Script for asking 'A' class clients for referrals:

"John and Mary, I really value the relationship that we've built up over the past five years of working with you. I wanted to let you know that we have been doing some planning in our firm and one of the things we've done is to categorize our clients to identify who are our ideal clients, and you're right up there on our top clients list. As I am sure you will know, most of our growth comes from referrals from existing clients and we'd really like to build the future of our firm around people like you. So assuming you're comfortable doing so, and that you're happy with the work we've been doing for you, we would really appreciate it if you happen to know anyone who might need an accounting firm like ours, if you could refer them to us."

Client education can be a major key here. Sometimes, your clients can get so caught up in running their own businesses that they are not fully aware of the work you have done together to help them achieve great results. In particular, they may not be able to articulate the approach you have taken with them. Never assume a client is 'worded up' to talk with potential referral candidates about the way you have worked together. Gently reminding your client of the way in which you have worked together can be helpful. Avoid the detail, but give consideration to priming the pump by pointing out some of the key points when you ask for referrals. For example:

> *'Sheila, when you're thinking of people who might benefit from the sort of work we have done together, it might help you to think about the first session we had where we worked together to identify the profit improvement potential in your business and then worked on where to focus attention to gather the low hanging fruit.'* Or, *'Bob, many of my best clients tell me that one of the most valuable parts of our business improvement work was the planning session. If you recall, you told me that was very helpful for you, as you had never set aside some serious time for planning before. You might know people who would really benefit from a similar session.'*

In summary, when building an accounting firm based on business improvement services, your client base is of critical importance. Take steps to ensure you are ultimately only working with the right sort of client. Remember, it's your business; you decide with whom you work.

3

Compliance as a springboard to business improvement

Compliance as a commodity

com·mod·i·ty /kə'mädiē/: a class of goods or services for which there is demand, but which is supplied without qualitative differentiation across a market.

Dress it up as much as you like, but compliance is rapidly becoming a commodity. A cursory glance through the short ads in your local newspaper will invariably turn up offers of 'cheap tax returns'. I just Googled 'tax return' and the top two entries were:

> Etax – 2011 Tax Return - Do your tax return on line now
> www.etax.com.au/TaxReturn2011
> **Tax returns** are easy at Etax.com.au
>
> Existing Users Login New Etax User
> Users Register   Feedback Tax Refund
> Now Double Your Tax Estimate Win an iPad
> Refund

> Express Tax Returns - Easier, Faster, Online Tax Returns.
> www.bcaccountants.com.au
> $44 Flat, Pay on **Refund**, All years.

Advances in technology have provided accountants with the means to significantly drive down the time taken to process compliance work. For the most part, accountants have been able to hold prices and I have seen the impact of this being manifested in lower write offs in the past few years.

As Bob Dylan might say, however, the times, they are a-changin'. The advent of Cloud-based accounting systems and the outsourcing of compliance work to Asia and other lower cost-base territories will likely drive processing time down even further, but this time, clients will cotton on. We are already seeing this happening. Recently I was in Auckland, New Zealand, and heard tell of one particularly progressive accounting firm that insists all of its clients move to Cloud accounting. The firm then outsources the processing of the work to Vietnam. They are very open with clients and prospects about the impact that this has on time and then they do what I believe is ethically the right thing to do – offer the work at lower prices than their competitors. The only team members they employ are senior accountants who spend most of their time nurturing clients and finding new opportunities. From the client's perspective, lower prices and increased client service equal a good deal.

We will see more and more of this sort of approach, resulting in downward price pressure for compliance-based services. Unless accountants embrace Cloud technology, aggressively promote it to their clients and then arm themselves to identify, sell and deliver value-based services, this movement has the power to wipe out a vast number of accounting firms.

There is also a move to simplify the tax system in many countries. In the country of my birth, the United Kingdom, a system of self assessment was introduced in the 1990s. If a tax payer receives a benefit, such as a company car, the employer informs the tax office, which in turn issues a revised coding number. The coding number adjusts the tax to be deducted from the employee's salary each month. The result is that the majority of tax payers do not need to file a tax return.

Similarly, when I started my career as an audit junior, virtually every incorporated business was required to have an audit. Now, the vast majority of businesses can claim audit exemption. Slowly but surely, the traditional accountant's heartland is being taken away.

In Australia, the compliance burden is still heavy but a simplified taxation system is constantly on the politicians' agenda. In the United States, the Department of Labor reported that in the 2005 fiscal year, over 134 million tax returns were filed (that number has no doubt increased since) all of which were due on 15th April. This annual filing frenzy can do nothing but create a sausage factory mentality. It's hard to even get to talk to an accountant between February and mid-April as they are all processing individual returns. On 16th April they fall in a heap, burnt out. The problem is, of course, that many US accountants make 80% of their profit in a couple of months, meaning they can then put their feet up for much of the rest of the year. This is not good for clients, who remain underserviced, or for accountants. Is this really how knowledge workers should be operating? Ultimately, change will occur via technology, legislation and price pressure.

The survey work we have done with clients shows consistently that clients change accountants for one or both of two reasons: lack of service and lack of services. To get stuck in the quagmire of compliance is to run the risk of client defection. As mentioned earlier, in 2000, the Goods and Services Tax (GST) was introduced in Australia.

The introduction of this tax was widely seen as being the goose that laid the golden egg for accountants – virtually every client would require more work to be done to bring them into compliance with the new tax. Yet what has actually happened is that accountants have been dragged even deeper into a web of even more low-value compliance. The result? More mind-numbing, tedious, processing work. And more disillusioned clients who continually pay accountants for services that they have to buy by law, rather than those that they choose to buy based on value.

So how to escape this web? I think it starts by looking for ways in which you can add value to your compliance work and in the process, differentiate your firm. The language you use can help; several firms with whom I work refer to their compliance work as *Business Essentials*, both internally and in client communications. I quite like that. However, I don't believe clients buy the fact that there is massive value in compliance on account of their ability to use their accounts for planning, benchmarking, refinancing, appeasing bankers, keeping them out jail and so forth. It is good to articulate these virtues but to truly grab your clients' attention, you need a different process.

How to add value to your core service

To truly add value to your compliance-based services you need to embrace an entirely new process. My recommendation is to integrate new processes that are low in labour intensity for you, yet high in value for your client – AND have the potential to identify new opportunities for you to work with your client in different ways.

Let's start at the very beginning. It is my view that before you start any job, you should have a discussion (preferably a face-to-face meeting) with the client to scope the job. At that meeting, you will determine if there are any changes to the scope of the job from last year (if it is an annual compliance job) and also to sell the value of what you are about to do. At that meeting, you have the perfect opportunity to apprise the client of a new approach that you will be implementing for your best clients. Try this script:

> *"John and Mary, as you know, we have your work booked in to start in two weeks' time. Before we get started on that, I thought it would be useful to outline for you a new approach that we are taking with our best clients this year. Our aim is to provide you with more value as we complete your year-end work. Would it be OK if I run through that with you now?*
>
> *Let me point out that there is no additional charge for the extras I am going to outline for you. It is part of our premium service to our best clients.*

> So, on top of simply completing your tax and accounts, this year we'll also do four things:
> 1. We will analyze your financial performance and provide you with graphs showing you the trends of your key numbers.
> 2. We will reconcile the profit number in your accounts to the movement in cash. We are often asked 'where did my cash go' so we will show you in an easy to understand way.
> 3. Once we are done, we will come out and meet with you and explain the accounts, then very importantly, work with you to set some preliminary targets for the next financial year.
> 4. I have assembled a task force of my best team members to brainstorm your business and I will bring you two or three ideas to improve your business."

What could the client possibly say in response to that other than something like 'that sounds terrific, look forward to seeing all of that.'? Note the importance of the language used. Reference to your 'best clients' indicates that this is not something you are doing for all and that this particular client is special. Take away the barriers by explaining there is no extra charge. Focus the client on value. And end with a promise to bring ideas to improve the client's business. It is a compelling value proposition from the client's perspective.

Easy enough to say, but how do you do that. Here are some ideas:

- **We will analyze your financial performance and provide you with graphs showing you the trends of your key numbers**

Instigate a policy whereby accountants cannot give a file to a partner without having completed an analytical review of the financial statements. I cannot stress the importance of this policy enough, on a number of levels (as such, this will not be the last time I recommend it in this book). The review should include a three-year trend analysis of the key profitability and liquidity ratios. Technology exists to crunch the numbers and display them in a way that makes sense to clients. The report at Figure 3.1 resonates well with clients because it displays the information in two different ways – numbers and pictures. Different people assimilate information in different ways and this enables you to engage your client, irrespective of their style, to educate them as to what is happening in their business.

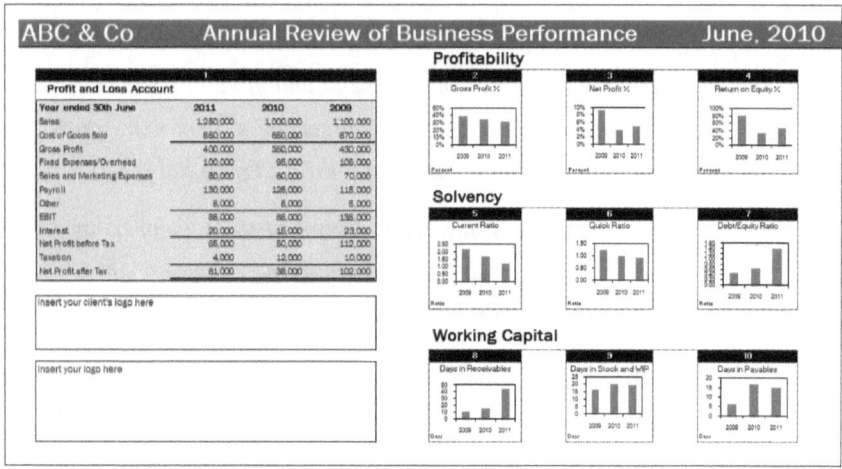

Figure 3.1: Annual Review of Business Performance

- **We will reconcile the profit number in your accounts to the movement in cash. We are often asked 'where did my cash go' so we will show you in an easy to understand way**

In my formative years as an accountant, most companies were required to have a Statement of Source and Application of Funds audited. Whilst this was yet another piece of compliance, when discussed with the client it was actually a useful document as it enabled the accountant to explain the difference between profit on the P&L account and cash movement during the year. Problem was, of course, that few accountants did any explaining and so the document remained a hidden treasure.

I prefer a simple approach and a graph is perfect for this purpose. Figure 3.2 provides an example. 10 minutes' work in Excel will give you the desired effect.

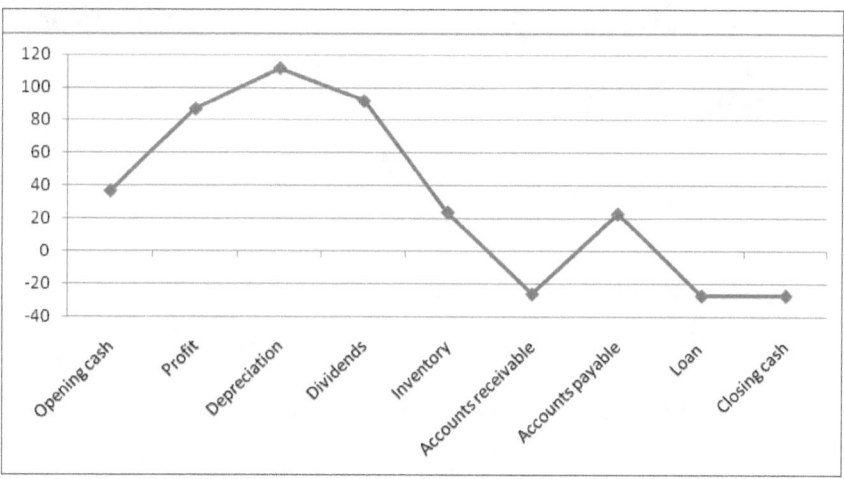

Figure 3.2 Where did my cash go?

- Once we are done, we will come out and meet with you and explain the accounts then very importantly, work with you to set some preliminary targets for the next financial year

I am a big believer in getting the client focused on top line improvements. By all means review costs but there is a limit to how much you can cut costs – to zero. And if you do so, you have no business. Yet the potential for top line improvement is endless and only constrained by cash flow. I will go deeper into how to work with clients to demonstrate profit improvement potential later in the book. For now, a simple equation such as that shown in Figure 3.3 is a superb conversation starter and enables you to set preliminary targets for the year ahead. It is also a huge eye-opener for clients. I have yet to meet a client who has not become engaged by this process. Clients rarely have the financial nous to consider their business potential in these terms and so few accountants ever have discussions like this, that you can be virtually assured it will be a brand-new experience of considerable value for your clients.

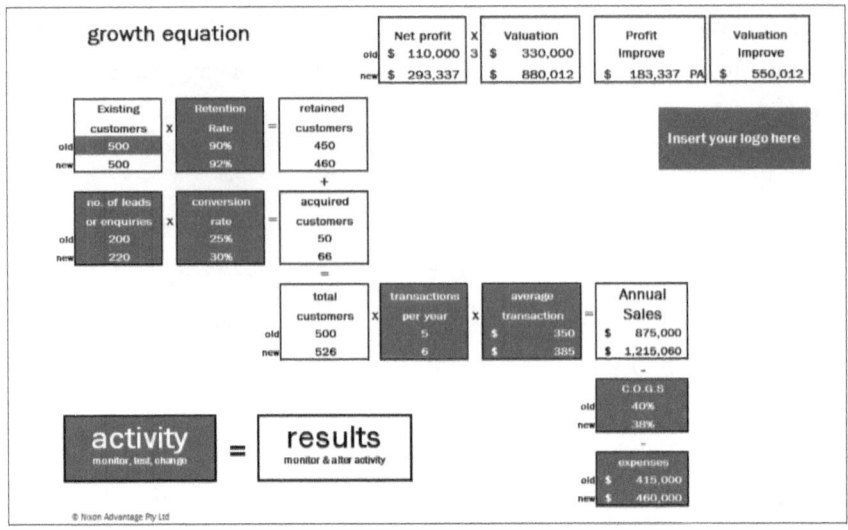

Figure 3.3 Target setting using a simple growth equation

- **I have assembled a task force of my best team members to brainstorm your business and I will bring you two or three ideas to improve your business**

In our Accountability Meetings with our members (all accounting firms) we run a learning module called Finding Opportunities. We ask each accountant to bring a set of client accounts with the names whited out. Working in groups, each person outlines the client's circumstances and answers questions from their group so that those who are not intimate with the client can gather more information. Then each group brainstorms the client for just 10 minutes to come up with ideas to improve the client's business. The key is to work quickly and not to over-analyze – simply flipchart all ideas. I guarantee that if you do this and get your team involved, you will come up with at least two ideas for your client every single time. Then all you need do is present them in the 'end of job' meeting and have a discussion around the ideas. Do this consistently and clients will receive tremendous value AND you will secure significant extra work. (Incidentally, the client's inference that you have mobilized some of your best team members on their behalf should not be underrated.)

The Annual General Meeting

We have worked with many accounting firms to formalise this approach through the facilitation of an Annual General Meeting to each business client. This is not only great practice (very few SME owners have formal Board or management meetings so the service has value in and of itself) but it also positions you as an integral part of the client's team. Refer back to Figure 1.2: if you want to become a Business Partner, rather than a Necessary Evil, you need more formalized contact with your clients.

Start with your 'A' class clients. As part of your client communication schedule, promise the facilitation of an AGM and get the time and date locked away in your and your clients' calendar. That way, it will happen. The four recommendations to differentiate your compliance work as noted above, provide the bones of the meeting agenda. I have included a sample agenda at Figure 3.4.

CLIENT NAME
ANNUAL GENERAL MEETING – AGENDA

1. Review of financial statements – discuss key points.
2. Tax payable – how much and when.
3. Review of trend analysis – 3 year review; key movements in trends
    a. Why have they occurred?
    b. What action is required?
4. Where did the cash go?
5. Looking forward – what is possible this year?
    a. Revenue planning.
    b. Key initiatives.

      c. Changes on the horizon.

      d. Ideas for business improvement.

6. Any other business – what is on your mind?

7. Next steps.

Figure 3.4: Annual General Meeting Agenda

The AGM is an obvious way to get your accountants more involved in face-to-face contact with clients. In Chapter 1, I referred to commercial acumen as a pre-requisite for an accountant interested in helping clients improve their business. But commercial acumen doesn't just happen. The best way to educate your senior accountants in how to conduct client interviews is to take them along to interviews with you. Originally as an observer, then as confidence develops, provide them with the freedom to ask a couple of pre-prepared questions. Consider two additional requirements expected of the accompanying accountant:

1. Prepare the agenda for the AGM, including key points of discussion from the analytical review and the business improvement ideas garnered from your team brainstorm.

2. Write a file memo of the meeting; summarizing the discussion, the client's reaction to any suggestions made and any follow up items agreed upon.

Logistically, it is important to be very organized as you start to offer AGMs. Once you have the meeting date in your calendar, your workflow system must swing into gear. It is your responsibility to ensure you have all of the information you need to process the work quickly so that you can meet your self-imposed deadline (the meeting date.) Having to constantly defer the AGM because you are waiting for information from the client will do nothing but frustrate the client. They will soon forget the great first impressions they held of this new approach. Remember, you are in control – if you have clients who are consistently hopeless at providing the information you need when you need it, these clients are not good candidates for your AGMs. Select those who have a track record of responsiveness; who do not cancel meetings on you; whom you have categorized as your better clients.

I recommend you allow 90 minutes for each AGM. This is a serious meeting and should be treated as such. Eliminate all distractions. If you know the client keeps getting dragged away if you meet on their premises, hold the meeting at your office and inform your team you are not to be disturbed. This also gives you the advantage of being on your own territory where you are in control of technology, the provision of refreshments and access to other team members for further information if required. But if you are going to hold the meetings in your office, make sure you have a clean, tidy and inspiring work environment in which to hold them.

You'll have noticed the final agenda item, being 'Next Steps'. Every time you hold a meeting with a client, there should be a definitive next step. Sometimes, a project will emerge there and then and your next step might be to summarize it in an implementation plan with some options and prices. You must agree with the client before you leave, as to *when* they will receive that plan, *when* they will read it and the *date and time* of your next meeting, or call to discuss it and choose which option they prefer. Other times, where no immediate project is apparent, simply book a meeting from a meeting. This is very simple to do:

> "Sheila and Bill, I have enjoyed our discussion today and I'm pleased you have everything covered just now. What I would like to do if it is OK with you is pop in to see you in three months' time. There will be no charge for that meeting; we have put in place performance standards in our firm to proactively meet with our best clients at least once a quarter just to touch base and ensure everything is under control. Can we put a date and time in the calendar right now for that next meeting?"

(Note – if they do not have their calendar to hand, let them know that your PA will be in touch to organize the next meeting.)

The AGM provides a safe haven to transition you up the value curve in your client's eyes. All business transactions are based on trust. You have immediate and implicit trust from your clients that you can do tax and accounting work (frankly, the client has no idea if what you have done is correct or not – they simply trust that it is). But you need to EARN trust to operate at a higher level with them. It is very difficult to jump straight into a business-planning session with a client if you have never engaged the client in discussions around their business performance before. The AGM provides a forum whereby you can position yourself perfectly for the next step up that value curve.

Leveraging into new opportunities

If you follow the process outlined in this chapter, you can't help but stumble across opportunities. The key is to listen intently to the client (stop thinking about what you are going to say next and focus 100% on the client) and then be prepared to step in and offer assistance when opportunities present themselves. Let's go through the differentiating value points and consider how we might leverage typical client responses into new work.

To frame this, note the agenda points I associated with the three-year trend analysis; why have variances in trends occurred and what action is required? I encourage you to pick out just two or three trends for discussion. Please avoid the temptation to discuss every single one in excruciating detail (unless you are dealing with an extremely analytical client). A typical conversation might emerge like this:

Example 1

You: If you look at this chart here you will see that your gross profit percentage has been declining. Two years ago it was tracking at 42%. Now it is running at 39%. What that means is for every $1,000 you sell, you are making $30 less than you were two years ago – and that's before you consider any increase in your general overhead over that time. Let me ask you a question – do you know why that has occurred?

Client: I have no idea.

You: Would it help to find out what has been going on here?

Example 2

You: If you look at this chart here you will see that your gross profit percentage has been declining. Two years ago it was tracking at 42%. Now it is running at 39%. What that means is for every $1,000 you sell, you are making $30 less than you were two years ago – and that's before you consider any increase in your general overhead over that time. Let me ask you a question – do you know why that has occurred?

Client: Yes. Our suppliers have increased their prices and we have been unable to pass on those increases to our customers.

You: How do you know that?

Client: What do you mean?

You: Well, have you attempted to pass on the price increases to your customers?

Client: Well, no, but I think we would lose a lot of customers if we did that.

You: Based on a gross profit percentage of 39%, if you increased you prices by 20% you could afford to lose more than one in three of your average customers and be no worse off. Do you really think you would lose that many?

Client: Probably not but we would need to do it very carefully.

You: That's where we can help. We can test price-increases progressively and monitor exactly what the results are. With any high-value customers whom you feel are price sensitive, we could set them aside in the first instance to manage the risk. Because we understand the numbers, we are very good at this sort of work and can provide you with a fresh pair of eyes on the whole situation.

Example 3

You: Many of our clients tell us that they don't understand where all the cash goes in their business. That's why we have prepared this simple chart to help you see the differences between profit on the P&L account and the movement in cash during the year.

Client: What can I draw from this?

You: Well, one thing that jumps off the page is your accounts receivable. There is over $40,000 more tied up in receivables than there was last year. Did you know that for a business of your size, just one extra day of your money being tied up with customers delaying payment to you, results in over $3,000 of free cash flow that you can't use? We have found in our business that by implementing strict receivables procedures and follow up processes, our days in receivables have dropped by 30% in the past 12 months, freeing up over $200,000 in cash flow for us. We can help you by implementing similar processes here. (IMPORTANT NOTE – before you say this you had better make sure your own receivables policy is rigorous and known to the client!)

Example 4

You: You did $1.2 million in revenue last year. If the stars were aligned and everything came together for you, what do you think you could achieve this year?

Client: Maybe $1.3 million at a push.

You: So that's an 8% increase in revenue. Which is around about what most of my clients start off thinking they could achieve. Interestingly, if you get really focused on the components of your revenue, being the number of customers, the number of times they buy from you each year and the average transaction value, I think you will agree that there is much more potential than you currently think for growing your business. I'd like to suggest we do some planning on that basis. Would you be open to that?

Client: By all means. Seriously, in this economy it would be hard to do more than 5-10% but let's take a look at your ideas.

Example 5

You: One of my best team members came up with an idea around your business structure. We have done some preliminary work on this and the potential tax savings are quite significant. Would you like me to explain what's at stake here and how we can work with you so that you can have those benefits?

Client: Fire away!

There are opportunities everywhere. You simply need to systematize your approach to uncovering them, present them in a way that makes sense to the client and then be bold and step into the breach when then client asks for your help. The more you do this, the better you will get at it. And the great thing is, the client is the real winner in all of these examples – and when that is the case, they will be more than happy to pay you for your contribution to the value they receive.

I strongly admonish you to be more aware of opportunities around you. When you are making notes in client or internal meetings, consider them with a view to how you could leverage ideas generated with other clients. When you attend seminars, rather than filing the workbook in the bin, go through and pull out the top 10 ideas as they relate to your clients – and progressively implement them. Remember also the golden rule; everything you implement to improve your own firm can then be taken and implemented with clients. We all need more awareness; if you regularly take bright ideas to your clients, they will be delighted and they will pay you to assist in the implementation of the ideas in which they see value.

I follow Seth Godin's blog (www.sethgodin.com) and recently saw an insightful entry that I feel reflects my sentiments in this chapter:

> 'Well rounded is like a resilient ball, rolling about, likely to be pleasing to most, and built to last.
>
> The opposite?
>
> Sharp.
>
> Sharp is often what we want. We don't want a surgeon **or an accountant** or even a tour guide to be well rounded. We have a lot of choices, and it's unlikely we're looking for a utility player.'

Systematize your systems and processes to become sharper in finding ways in which you can differentiate your core services AND help your clients build their businesses.

4

Turning wants into needs

Why 'knee-jerking' is costing you serious money

Accountants spend way too much time being reactive and nowhere near enough time being proactive. After years of observing the way in which accountants work, my conclusion is that this is not because they don't want to be proactive; it simply emerges as the firm grows.

If you are a partner, think back to when you started, acquired, bought into or inherited your accounting firm. I am willing to bet that your behaviour was very different back then. If the phone rang, you would grab it in your desperation for new business. Weren't you asking everyone you knew for referrals, letting them know that you were on the lookout for new clients? (And guess what, new clients came!) And I am also sure that you spent more time with existing clients in the hope of identifying opportunities for additional work.

But then something happened that changed your working style. The firm grew and you got too busy. And now, if you are like the majority of accountants, you cringe when the phone rings. You have no time for networking. You worry about visiting clients in case you bring back more work. And when a client calls to ask a question, your instinct is to give it to them quickly to get them off the phone so that you can get back to the pressing issue you were working on.

This is a cycle that will wind up with you feeling stressed, frustrated and underpaid. Your modus operandi has become the knee jerk. And knee-jerk responses are in neither your, nor your clients' best interests.

You'll recall our proposition that a partner in an accounting firm should only be doing three things - high value chargeable work for 600 hours a year tops; client nurturing; and leadership / strategy development. One of the fundamental reasons we advocate you drive your chargeable time DOWN as a partner is so that you have the time to get out of the knee-jerk habit.

Prescription without diagnosis is malpractice. You wouldn't accept it from your doctor. Imagine if you went in with a pain in your stomach and the doctor dismissed you in 30 seconds with a script for some tablets. That is essentially tantamount to what you are doing when you hurry a client off the phone with the advice to 'just do this.' But to help clients in a way that they deserve, you must help yourself first.

CASE STUDY

Michael is a sole practitioner in a fast-growing firm. He has doubled his fees in two years and has work coming out of his ears. When he acquired the business it was predominantly a tax-return shop with a few business clients. Michael soon got bored with preparing tax returns in front of the client. What he really wanted to do was to get involved in helping his business clients. But to do that, he had to stop doing some of the things he was doing to make time to do the things he really wanted to do.

His first step was to list everything that he personally was doing. He did this over a three-week period until trends started to emerge. He then determined to delegate all low value and administrative tasks. But of course, as is typical in a small firm, he had no one to delegate to, as everyone else was busy. So Michael hired a professional PA. He was astonished how much he was able to delegate to his PA and how much of his time he was able to free up.

With his new-found time, Michael visited all of his business clients and was able to upgrade 60% of them to quarterly meetings (previously they were all once a year clients.) He also developed and nurtured relationships with local bank managers. As a result, he has a steady stream of referrals from both clients and bankers. He still has work coming out of his ears but it is the right sort of work and he is loving the fact that he is now making a serious difference with his clients.

Case in point; to help your clients you must first help yourself.

So to stop knee jerking, it is important to address the cause, not the symptom itself. What is causing this behaviour? And what do you need to put in place to find more time for yourself so that you can do the things you want - and operate in line with your clients' best interests? You may need to do what Michael did and hire a PA. Or perhaps you need to become better at delegating. Or maybe you need to spend that $100,000 on a quality senior accountant to take on some of the load. What is it for you?

Consider this; if every day you receive two inbound phone calls from clients asking for advice that you respond to with a quick, knee-jerk response, and assuming you bill in arrears based on time and you remember to put a couple of units on the time sheet at say $300 per hour, over the course of a year you will charge approximately $27,000 to WIP in respect of these phone calls. But what if by eliminating the knee jerk, 50% of those phone calls could have transpired into new projects at an average price of $5,000? That's a million dollars a year you could be leaving on the table. Worse still, how much value have your clients potentially lost as a result of your response? THAT, in my view, is the real issue at stake here.

It is in your clients' best interests to ignore what they say

In February 2011, I read an article in Time Magazine about Singularity. My understanding of the article was that by 2045, it is expected that computers will 'catch up' with the human brain. I have absolutely no idea what that means for humanity. It sounds scary yet exciting at the same time, but for me it is impossible to conceptualize the outcome.

And that is a critically important point to get. We (as in you, me, your clients, people at large) do not know what we don't know.

In my career to date I have facilitated 71 client advisory boards for accounting firms. A client advisory board is an excellent process, involving the accountant inviting 10 to 12 of their best clients to a two hour meeting, facilitated by an independent chair, to gather input from the clients on what the firm does really well, where it needs to improve and for the clients to proffer suggestions in terms of additional services that they would find valuable.

From a client nurturing and client service perspective a client advisory board is a very worthwhile activity. But I can count on the fingers of one hand across the 71 meetings the number of innovative suggestions given by clients in terms of new services or service extensions. You see, people don't know what they don't know.

Steve Jobs was fond of saying that it is pointless to ask customers for suggestions for future innovation. If he had asked mobile phone users what they needed to make their phones even better it is inconceivable to imagine that he would have received feedback that would have led to what we now know as the iPhone. Similarly, who had any idea that compact discs would be a better solution than vinyl? (Some would argue they are not!) What customer could conceive the idea of a 5cm square, lightweight dongle that could plug into your laptop and provide 4G wireless Internet speed of up to 100Mbps?

Verne Harnish, in his book *Mastering the Rockefeller Habits,* encourages business owners to ask themselves what is their customers' greatest need? He goes on very specifically to delineate between needs and wants, saying that customers will 'want, want, want you all the way to bankruptcy if you let them!' Good point.

In my accounting days, I delivered many planning sessions to clients and I have since helped other accountants roll out that service to their clients. I can tell you that not once did a client ever approach me and say 'I need a planning session.' Indeed, when I pushed back against what they said they wanted and suggested that in fact they *needed* a planning session, there was sometimes a certain level of scepticism. And yet 100% of the time, the clients reported after the session that it was of great value. In fact, I have heard more than once after running a planning session that 'this was just what we needed.' But no-one knew that beforehand.

This is why I posit that it is in your clients' best interests that you disregard what they say they want. It is not their fault – they simply don't know any better. But if you accept what they say they want to be what they actually need, you are doing your clients (and yourself) a disservice.

Let me give you a couple of examples. Here's one you will almost certainly relate to. A client calls, while standing in a car showroom. They are about to buy the car and want to know if they should put it on hire purchase or lease. The knee-jerk reaction is to give them an answer on the spot. Accountants tell me that in that situation it is impossible to do otherwise. Really? How many clients would object if you said that you needed to ask them some questions to gather more information so that you could be sure that your answer was in their best interests from a tax-minimization perspective? And that once you had considered their responses, you would go back to them with a formal letter of advice – price for the work, $450. I think you are doing your clients a disservice if you knee-jerk and give them an ill-considered response just to get them off the phone. I know you are doing it because they are standing in the showroom and want to make a decision but realistically, they can't take the car away that instant in most cases; what difference will another day make to ensure all the ducks are lined up?

Here is another, perhaps familiar, example. I recall a client, John, calling me to say he needed a cash flow forecast. In my work with hundreds of accounting firms around the world, I know categorically that in 90% of cases, the conversation would go something like this:

John:	*I need a cash flow forecast.*
Accountant:	*Fine, we can do that. When do you need it by?*
John:	*How much will it cost?*
Accountant:	*Well, that depends on how long it takes us to complete the work.*
John:	*You must have a ballpark figure.*
Accountant:	*It's usually around $1,500.*
John:	*Goodness me, that's a lot of money. We are really tight on cash. Couldn't you do it for less just this once?*
Accountant:	*OK, we'll do it for $900 for you. So when do you need it?*
John:	*Straight away. The bank is putting us under pressure.*
Accountant:	*That's fine. We will drop everything and get right onto it for you.*

There are all sorts of things wrong with this discussion. The client is in control of a situation that the accountant should own. The accountant has caved on price and hence set the benchmark for all future price negotiations. The accountant has volunteered to bump other presumably important clients' work in exchange for a $900 fee which will no doubt have very little profitability attached to it. But most importantly, the accountant has agreed to do this work without finding out what the client REALLY needs. And that smacks of negligence to me.

Let's turn this discussion around:

John: I need a cash flow forecast.

Accountant: Thank you for calling, John. Tell me, why do you need a cash flow forecast?

John: The bank told us we had to get one done.

Accountant: Is that right? Do you know why they need a cash flow forecast from you?

John: We couldn't afford the wages last week so I approached the bank manager for an extension of the overdraft.

Accountant: Really. Do you know what happened to put you in the situation where you couldn't afford the wages?

John: That's a good question. You know, I have been getting concerned that sales seem to be declining.

Accountant: Is that right. Would it help to take a look at why that might be happening?

John: Could you do that? That would be incredibly helpful.

Accountant: We can certainly do that. But first, let me talk with the bank manager before we rush into preparing any forecasts. Who do you deal with?

John: Mary Anderson at Westpac.

Accountant: I know Mary well. Let me give you a call on your behalf and then I'll call you straight back and we'll get a plan together from there.

Now in this situation, the accountant may or may not end up doing the cash flow forecast but if they do, it will be on their terms. The entire discussion is more focused on the client and begins to uncover what the client really needs. The accountant is not there yet and I will expand on how to dig deeper to establish real needs and objectives. But this discussion is in a much better place. Imagine how the client FEELS after this discussion versus the previous one. It would be difficult to argue that this approach is not in the client's best interests. And that needs to be the yardstick by which we measure our approach and our actions.

The ultimate question to use every time

As accountants, we are trained to be the experts. Many accountants are also analytical by nature; we like facts, figures, logic and process. This training results in some challenges, and I believe, is a primary reason for the knee jerk. Oftentimes we believe we know the answer straight away and given that, why search for anything else?

When in the realms of a technical challenge, it is fine to know the answer and be able to expedite a quick response. After all, your client deserves the fastest resolution to their issues that you can possibly come up with. Once we move out of technical-land, however, the goal posts move. To find the most appropriate solution for the client, we need to move far away from our comfort zone of 'what' and 'how' and consistently ask the ultimate question that will get to the real issues at hand. That question is WHY.

As I demonstrated in the previous example, constantly digging deeper by asking why or a variant thereof, moves you from hearing what the client thinks they need to what they truly need. Sound simple? It is - but it is not a comfortable place for accountants and as such, it needs some work.

Yet, we are born with the ability to ask why. Anyone with young children will know all too well how they drive you crazy by forever asking why, why, why, why, why! They do this for a reason; they have a thirst for knowledge and they genuinely do not know the answer. For these reasons, asking why comes easy to them. 'Daddy, why did is that green arrow flashing?' 'Because I put the indicator on.' 'What's the indicator?' 'This lever here.' 'Why did you put the lever on?' 'Because we needed to turn left?' 'Why are we going left?' 'Because Brisbane is in that direction and that's where we are going.' 'Why are we going to Brisbane?' And on it goes. By the end of it, you are tearing your hair out but your child has acquired new knowledge and uncovered the real reason the green arrow on the dashboard was flashing.

It's often said that there is no such thing as a stupid question. I am not sure that is 100% correct as I have heard some pretty dumb questions in my time, but during the diagnosis with your client, lots of questions is a good thing. You might instantly know the answer to the client's issue but it behoves you and the client to dig deeper.

Another reason why you should ask why more often is to uncover the reason behind the reason. Take the simple example of a retail client, let's call her Margaret, who approaches you to discuss a plan to open a new shop. The knee-jerk response, of course, would be to do the business plan, cash flow, get involved in raising finance, ensuring the structure is beneficial and so on. But if you jump straight to solutions, what might you miss? What if the discussion panned out like this:

Margaret:	*We have decided to open a new shop in Sydney.*
You:	*That's interesting. Tell me more. Why are you doing that?*
Margaret:	*We're just not making enough money here in Brisbane.*
You:	*Why do you need more profit?*
Margaret:	*The shop's doing OK, but Jack and I have the kids' school fees to think about in a few years' time and we are concerned we won't be able to cover them with our current level of profitability.*
You:	*What else is concerning you?*

Margaret:	We haven't been able to afford a proper holiday for four years and frankly it is causing some real tension between us.
You:	Is there anything else you are worried about?
Margaret:	No, they are the main issues on my mind.
You:	When you opened the shop in Brisbane, where did you hope you would be by now in terms of profitability?
Margaret:	I genuinely thought we would be making $250,000 a year. We are nowhere near that.
You:	Why do you think that is?
Margaret:	I really don't know. We just can't put our finger on it.
You:	So can I ask, why do you think opening another shop in Sydney would solve the problems you are having in Brisbane?
Margaret:	Do you know, we haven't really asked ourselves that question. I guess Jack and I just assumed we need to increase sales and that is one way of doing it. Do you think there might be a better way?
You:	Margaret, if it's OK with you, here is what I propose we do. Let's set some time aside and do some proper planning on this. I would like to work with you and Jack to help you understand the key drivers of revenue and profitability in your shop. It may be that there are some opportunities to increase revenue and profit in Brisbane by trying some different things. Right now, we don't know. It may transpire that opening another shop turns out to be exactly the right thing to do but knowing the hard costs associated with that and the difficulties involved in managing multiple locations, I think it is worth at least considering an alternative approach. How does that sound to you?

There is nothing magical about this approach. No silver bullet. All you are doing is showing a genuine interest in your client and putting forward a suggestion that is in line with their interests. Every accountant in the world can do this. But few do because they jump to solutions. Bite your tongue, listen, breathe and ask why. You will be amazed at where that simple question takes you and your clients.

Articulating value so that everyone wins

The only way to truly articulate value is for the client to do it. The somewhat hackneyed phrase 'the client has all the answers – your role is to facilitate' is all very well but in my experience, most accountants need some guidance in how to facilitate the extraction of those answers and then turn them into statements of value.

In this section, I draw heavily on the work of a man who has influenced me greatly since I was introduced to his work in 2007, Alan Weiss, the consultant's consultant. We have brought Alan out to Australia three times to speak at our conferences and many accountants in our network are using his value pricing philosophies. Visit Alan's website, www.summitconsulting.com for free articles and downloads and subscribe to his blog, www.contrarianconsulting.com. Put simply, Alan is quite possibly the smartest human being I have ever met and you will benefit enormously from immersing yourself in Alan's work.

When I observe the leading rainmakers in the accounting profession, they almost always (subconsciously or not) follow a process very much aligned with Alan's recommendations. I was the co-developer of a Cloud-based tool that systematically enables accountants to ask the right questions in the right order, every single time, no matter who in the firm drives the tool. The results are very predictable – in virtually every case the client ends up with an action plan that they have agreed to and prioritised and the accountant gets involved with helping the client implement the plan. The reason I developed that tool with my then business partner, Shannon Vincent (pre-Alan, incidentally) was to address a clear need in that so few accountants follow any process to determine client needs.

In our Accountability Meetings we educate accountants using role plays and case studies in a proven process that, when followed, results in the client articulating to you the value they see in achieving the objectives that they have determined. That is the key. Figure 4.1 shows the order in which you should ask questions to get the best outcome.

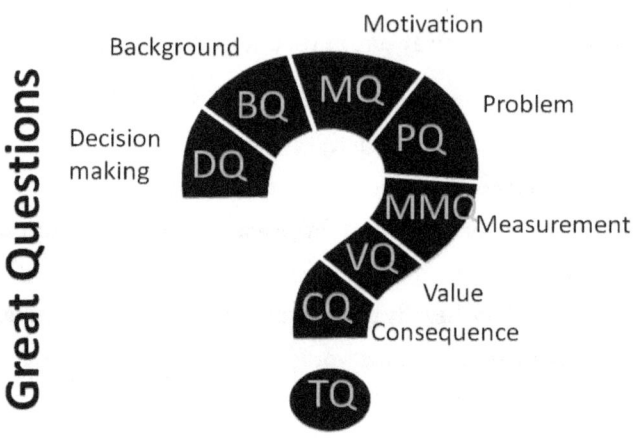

Figure 4.1 Great questions to wind up with a great outcome

Alan talks about objectives, measures and values and refers to a conceptual agreement having been reached once you have worked with the client to agree upon them. In our model above, the objectives are covered by the MQ and PQ questions – what is motivating the client to want to do this and what are the problems that are stopping the desired state being achieved right now? For a good, meaty project you are looking for four or five strong objectives which you determine by asking the 'why' questions as outlined above. Once the client specifies that there is nothing else, summarise the discussion thus far in the following way:

> *Chris, let me summarise if I may. What we are talking about here are four specific objectives, being:*
> 1. *You would like to make more profit, and specifically, you would like your profit to increase from $120,000 to $300,000.*
> 2. *When you achieve that level of profitability, we agreed that the value of the business when you come to sell it would be worth significantly more, likely to be in the region of an additional $500,000.*
> 3. *You said that with that amount of extra profit you would like to build up your retirement plan by investing an extra $50,000 per year into it so that you can retire gracefully at the age of 60.*
> 4. *And finally you explained that you would like to see a structure in your business whereby you could take six weeks leave each year and the business would go on without you being there.*
>
> *Is that a fair reflection of our discussion?*

The client can either say no, there is something else, or number 3 is not quite right, let's get that nailed down, or yes, that covers it. Once there is nothing else and the client is happy, move to measures. To determine the measures, ask the client:

> *How would you know that we are on track towards achieving those objectives? Let's start with the first one – increased profitability.*

Work through each objective and get a measure for each. A key to remember is that you are looking for short term metrics to show progress towards longer term goals. For example, metrics in this case might be:

Objective	Measure (as articulated by the client)
You would like to make more profit, and specifically, you would like your profit to increase from $120,000 to $300,000.	If we can get to, say, $170,000 in year one and feel as though we are making continual progress, that would be great.
If we can do that, we agreed that the value of the business when you come to sell it would be worth significantly more, likely to be in the region of an additional $500,000.	Let's get a valuation done now and another in 12 months' time. If value is increasing, we are on the right track.
You said that with that amount of extra profit you would like to build up your retirement plan by investing an extra $50,000 per year into it so that you can retire gracefully at the age of 60	If I can put anything extra into my retirement plan this year I would be delighted.
And finally you explained that you would like to see a structure in your business whereby you could take six weeks leave each year and the business would go on without you being there.	In six months' time I would like to have identified a general manager for the business, either from the team we have now or someone external whom we could bring in.

Once you have the measures, move straight to value. To ascertain the client's perception of value, simply ask:

What would the impact be on you, on your business and on your family of achieving all of these objectives?

And let the client answer. There are no wrong or right answers. You may need to guide the client to keep them on track. Make sure you have at least one statement of value for each objective and write down EXACTLY what the client says. Once the client has finished, you have your objectives, measures and values as specified by the client. Beautifully articulated, in their words and with their priorities. Now all you have to do is work as a business partner with your client to deliver upon some very clearly defined objectives and your client will be delighted to pay you a value-based fee.

The biggest mistake I see in this area is accountants making assumptions on behalf of the client to come up with the objectives, measures and values. In their excitement at having the opportunity to propose on a business improvement project, they move too quickly. Every time I am asked to critique a proposal or implementation plan, the first question I ask is 'who came up with the objectives? You or the client?' It must be the client. By all means, guide them with subtle questions but the words need to come out of their mouth. If it takes you three meetings to get to that point, so be it – it is worth the wait because the outcome will be far superior for both you and your client.

As a case in point, as I type this, a message has just appeared on our Cloud-based forum through which we connect accountants to share ideas. One of our members, Christian, followed this precise process and has signed up a $57,000 tax advisory project. To quote Christian: 'The best thing was the client and I went for a beer after signing on the dotted line - both very happy with our win for the day!' And that is what this is all about; everyone's happy – great deal.

5

Showing clients what is possible in their businesses

The power of language

Never underestimate the importance of the language you use in client meetings. I see a primary purpose of any client meeting being to open your clients' eyes to the opportunities that are lying dormant in their business. As an accountant, you owe it to yourself and your clients to get much better at helping clients understand what is possible. And that is **all** in the language.

Here are some examples of great questions that can transform a meeting from mundane to magnificent:

- Opening a meeting with a prospect who has attended a seminar: "Why did you come along to the seminar?" Followed by: "What was the number one idea you took away from the seminar?" Then: "How do you plan to implement that idea?"

- Gathering background from a client or prospect: "When you started/bought/inherited this business, where did you hope you would be by now?"
- Transitioning to helping clients define their objectives: "Where would you like the business to be in three years' time?"
- Upon discovering an objective – say, to make more profit: "How much more? What would you do with the extra money?" Will help uncover deeper objectives – and likely the REAL objectives.
- Upon determining a lifestyle objective – for example, to travel for six months: "What would need to be in place for that to happen?" "Who will look after your business while you are away?" "What's your time frame to make this happen?" "How much extra profit do you need to generate in the business to fund this?"
- To help the client understand the value accruing to them of working towards their objectives: "What would be the impact if we were to work together to do this? On you, your business, your family?"
- When you think you have all of the objectives, measures, or points of value: "Is there anything else?"
- When asked 'which option should I choose': "Our best clients choose option 3."
- If the client asks you to sell them on why they should do this: "You should do it if YOU want to. So let's talk about what you are looking to achieve."

You need to master the language. Practice regularly, with your team, your family, but more importantly, with your clients. The more you get in front of them in real life situations, the better you will become at helping them understand the opportunities that lie before them. If you have never had a conversation with your client around their business goals before, some will be naturally suspicious and that suspicion often manifests itself in the form of objections. Here are some more scenarios to help you master the language required to turn around some of the primary objections you may face.

Scenario 1: You (the accountant) have set up a meeting with your client. You have no plans to charge for the meeting but the client is suspicious. 'What's this all about? What is it going to cost me?'

Wrong language: 'Erm... I'm sorry, we should have let you know that before. It's a free meeting. I just wanted to make sure that everything has been covered.'

Correct language: 'We've implemented a policy to meet up with our best business clients at least three times a year at no cost. Our goal is to help you understand the potential in your business and assist you in setting ambitious yet achievable goals and objectives. So tell me, where would you like your business to be in three years' time?'

Scenario 2: You have identified that a client has very seasonal cash flow and feel that a working cash flow and budget would benefit the client.

Wrong language: We have bought some new software and can create a cash flow that will help you.

Correct language: I'm conscious of the fact that your business is very seasonal. How easy does that make it to manage your cash flow? Do you know the impact on your cash flow of reducing your accounts receivable days by 10 days? One thing we notice with our clients is that revenue growth can put strain on cash flow. Would you be interested in taking a look at the impact of that and looking at some sensitivity analysis? If we could help you smooth out the seasonality of your cash flow so that you have more certainty around your cash inflows and outflows, what impact would that have on you and your business?

Scenario 3: You have opened a new office in a smaller town 20km from where you are based. You have secured a meeting with one of the more influential business people in the new town. She is sceptical as to why she should work with you.

Wrong language: We can do it cheaper.

Correct language: We are not the cheapest but there is a reason for that. The way we work is more in-depth than a traditional accountant. Because we have access to more resources, we are able to offer a range of additional services that add significant value to our clients. Would you like to explore how that external perspective might help you?

When I say 'correct' language, take the concept and then apply your style to it. Focus on your client and how you can help them; constantly work on your language and practice it. The more you do this, the better you will get and the more value you will add to your clients' business and your own.

Another smart concept to embrace is that a picture paints a thousand words. I find it no surprise that those accountants I see having great success with business-improvement work with clients are regularly varying the way in which they communicate ideas to their clients. Jumping up to draw a diagram or a graph on a whiteboard can cement the point you are trying to make and enable a client to suddenly 'get it.' Become practised at these; pull together a small number of charts, diagrams and other visuals that you can reproduce as required in the moment. It is much more powerful to draw them than to pull up a PowerPoint slide. In the absence of a whiteboard, an application such as Noteshelf allows you to draw on the screen of your iPad – very powerful in a client meeting.

I favour four quadrants to make a point. These can be portrayed in the form of a double axis graph, demonstrating the preferred position based on two criteria (see Figure 1.1 in this book for an example.) Or more simply, four quadrants enables focus on four key aspects of any particular strategy. I like the question 'if you could pick just four areas that you have to get absolutely right, what would they be?' There is no magic to the number four, but it seems to work in terms of the diagram.

As an example of this – one slightly out of left field – we recently bought our children a whiteboard and markers to scribble on at home. My eight-year-old son, Matthew, apparently inspired by a diagram he found on my desk that I had been working on for this book, came up with four components that in his view business owners should focus on. I reproduce the diagram at Figure 5.1 to make the point.

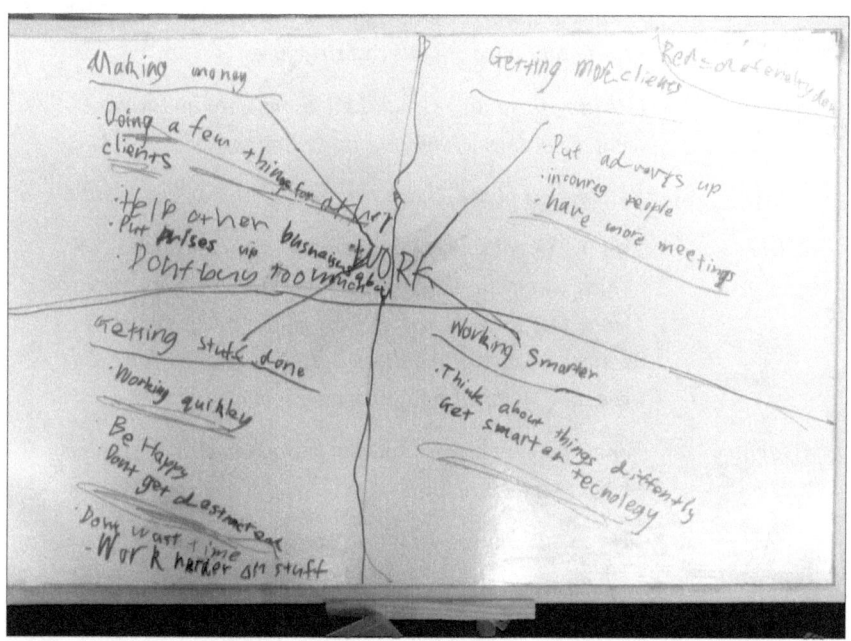

Figure 5.1 How to get the most out of work, according to my eight-year-old, Matthew, skilled in the art of using whiteboards and diagrams!

Excuse the spelling and handwriting but I feel it does make the point so beautifully well. Imagine the discussion with a client:

> YOU: Tim, if you could focus on just four things to get right next year, what would they be?
>
> TIM: We need to make more money; get some more clients; get some 'stuff' done – we have projects sitting around that we are not finishing; and finally find ways to work smarter.
>
> YOU: (Writing them on a chart on the whiteboard as Tim speaks) Fantastic. Let's take each one in turn. What ideas do you have in each quadrant?

TIM:	*Let's start with making money. We've got a strong customer base and we should be offering more to them. There are also many people out there who don't know about the great things we are doing with our customers so we need to get the word out to them. Also, I think we should review our pricing. Oh, we're also spending way too much money. We need to take a look at our cost structure.*
YOU:	*(Writing them up.) Great. Let's move onto quadrant 2 – what ideas do you have around getting new clients?*
TIM:	*Responds as above...then work through quadrants 3 and 4*
YOU:	*Tim, we've got four or five great ideas in each area here. Which would be the 'must do' ideas in each quadrant? (Underline them in red as Tim gives you his thoughts – Matthew's label on the chart – 'Red = definitely do.' Kids have such an instinctive grasp on implementation!)*
YOU:	*What you have here is a focused plan for next year. Has this been a useful exercise?*
TIM:	*Very useful. Do you know, no accountant has ever spoken with me about my business in these terms before?*
YOU:	*How confident are you that you can implement that on your own?*
TIM:	*I would really value some help. Perhaps we need to meet with you more frequently...*

The power of the conversation is in the diagram. It provides a framework, real focus and a start and end point. And if my eight year old can come up with this, I am confident you can too.

Do this simple calculation:

Incremental amount currently being left on the table per business client group because of sub-optimal language x number of business client groups = annual $ left on the table. Then multiply that number by the number of years you have run your business. You can never get that money back – but you can start today to make sure the issue does not blow out any further.

The power of numbers

In the past decade there has been a trend for business owners to hire coaches to provide guidance and strategic input. Unfortunately many businesses have been poorly advised by coaches who simply don't understand the numbers. Without a solid grasp of the key drivers of revenue and profit and the importance of working capital management, an advisor can end up in dangerous territory. This is why accountants are the true, trusted advisors (when they step up and embrace the role.)

Most business owners significantly underestimate what is possible in their businesses. Their growth plans are incremental because they have not been enlightened as to the true potential.

The first thing I want to know when looking at the potential to improve a business is what are the components of the business's revenue. I operate by the mantra that as soon as you show the client something they did not previously know, you are adding serious value. I have met very few business owners who could tell you precisely how many customers they have. As such, this is a great discussion to have with any client.

In a generic business (one with regular customers who transact several times a year) the revenue components are as follows:

- Number of customers.
- Retention rate.
- Number of enquiries or leads.
- Conversion rate to new customers.
- Average number of transactions per customer per year.
- Average transaction value.

To help your client understand the growth potential, the key is to break down the revenue into these various components so that you can determine where most leverage resides to grow the top line. The way to do this is to ask the client a series of questions:

> *'John and Mary, your revenue last year was $2 million. What do you think you might be able to increase that to this year if we get really focused on growth?'*

Most clients will respond with a small increase (5 or 10%). Simply listen to the client's response and then ask:

> *'Do you know where you need to focus to achieve that growth?'*

In most cases, the client will not have a firm plan in mind. And this is where you transition them into revenue planning.

> *'Our observation in working with our clients has been that if we can help you get very focused on the key drivers of revenue, that provides real focus around the strategies required to grow. Would you like me to explain how we might do that?'*

You then step into a series of questions to help the client understand the potential. I like to start with the number of customers. Quite simply:

> *'Tell me, how many active customers do you have right now?'*

Most clients will not know. Some will have an idea. Often, if you are at the client's premises or have access to the client's accounting system, you can run a sales report by customer to get an approximation. Do not overanalyse. You are looking for numbers that are close enough to work with.

In some cases (retail, for example) the client will have no way of tracking each discrete customer. In that case, look for the total number of transactions. You can usually find this on till roll summaries.

Next, ask the client what proportion of customers they typically lose during the year. Again, an approximation is fine. If the client has no idea, suggest that it's your experience that where there is no focused retention program in place, businesses tend to lose between 10 and 20% of customers, so work with 10%.

Now move to new customers. How many enquiries does the client receive each month? And what is the conversion rate? Often clients will overestimate this number so this is a good opportunity to pre-frame for the client that as you start to work together more closely, you will help them implement a measurement system so that they know exactly what the numbers are. I use the line that if you don't know your starting point, it is impossible to plan properly.

Next, move onto the average transaction frequency. How many times per year does your average customer buy from you? And finally, average transaction value. This number is often the critical one.

You can run these calculations using planning software, a spreadsheet or on the back of an envelope. You will find that you may sometimes be missing one piece of data (for example, the number of customers) but if you ascertain the number of transactions and the average transaction value and you get an approximation for the transaction frequency, the missing number will pop out as a balancing figure.

The first client I worked with on a business improvement engagement happened to be a retailer (a baker). Based on figures we were able to obtain from the client's system and his approximation of average transaction frequency, we estimated that he had 56,000 discrete customers. We were able to show him that by increasing the average transaction value by just 10 pence, £63,000 would drop to the bottom line. You'll find that with high volume, average transaction value is often the key. This gave the client immediate focus and we worked together to test and implement ideas that would drive that critical KPI.

Not all businesses fit this generic model. For example, I worked with a light engineering business where the revenue components were jobs quoted, % won and average job value. We also worked with a firm of lawyers where it was all about client retention, lead generation and conversion, number of projects per client and average project value (incidentally, these KPIs apply to your accounting firm as well).

As an accountant, numbers are your strength. Stay close to them. You have instant credibility in any numbers-based discussion and you can add serious value to the client by opening their eyes to the growth opportunities using this approach. Bear in mind that if you can help the client increase net customers by 10%, increase average transaction frequency by 10% and average transaction value by 10%, revenue will grow by 33%. This will almost always be significantly more than the client thought possible at the start of the discussion. And this is the value you bring to the table.

CASE STUDY

One of our members was working with a beauty salon in a small town. Their reputation had flourished to the point where they were overwhelmed with work. The business owner, although now making good money, was working stupid hours and had decided to close the business as a knee-jerk way out, knowing she could get a no-stress job doing her thing for someone else.

Her accountant got her focused on the numbers and demonstrated that if she increased her prices by 30% she could afford to lose half of her customers and still make the same amount of money. This was a complete eye-opener. Her biggest frustration was having too many customers but it had never occurred to her that she could lose some of them and be better off. And if none of them left after the price increase, she could easily afford to hire an assistant to take some pressure off her.

Enabling clients to discover for themselves

To gain true buy-in from your client, you must engage them in the discovery process. Because you understand numbers, the answer to the client's growth conundrum could well be obvious to you. But to optimize the outcome, resist the temptation to jump straight to that answer. With my baker, some cursory analysis before we met with the client indicated strongly where the answer would be. I am convinced that had I simply TOLD the client that he needed to focus on average transaction value, the result would have been very different. You see, when clients discover for themselves, they are engaged.

Let me give you an example. Imagine you are sitting with a client and you determine that the current average transaction value is $250. There are two ways to move the conversation forward from there. Firstly, what I am going to suggest is the wrong way:

'Graham, let's increase that to $270 and see what the impact is.'

The problem is that this is your number, not the client's. They will rarely argue with the number but they will not buy into it. Here's an alternative - and, I suggest, much more effective - approach:

YOU: *'Graham, if we got really focused on improving that number, what do you think you might be able to increase it to?'*

GRAHAM: *'We could probably get that up to $300.'*

YOU: *'What if it was just half of that - say $275. Do you think you could achieve that?'*

GRAHAM: *'Absolutely. Let's go with that.'*

There is a huge difference between these two approaches. In the first example, the $270 was your number and the client's response, whether expressed or not, is doubt as to whether it can be achieved. In the second example, the client 'owns' the $275 and, in fact, feels it is a conservative target because he originally suggested $300.

This is not trickery. I have found that it pays to be conservative when setting targets for three reasons:

1. For true engagement, the client has to believe it is achievable.
2. If you reel in unrealistic or even ambitious targets, the client understands you are not trying to use smoke and mirrors to make the number look good.

3. You know that even a 10% increase in each variable is going to have a dramatic impact on revenue, so there is no need to go any higher for the purpose of the exercise.

In our work with accountants, we set targets for rolling 90-day periods. We have learnt from experience that we must let our members (the accountants) set their own targets. We are often asked for guidance as to what the target should be but other than encouraging the member to be bold and aim high, we pull back from suggesting a number. The primary reason for this is accountability. If I set the target for the member, the member has an excuse if it is not achieved – 'that was your target; I never believed we could achieve it.' But if you set the target, you have no excuses and the accountability to the achievement of the target is much stronger.

Some accountants have found that if using software or a spreadsheet to demonstrate the profit improvement potential, even more engagement can be gained by having the client type in the target for each variable themselves. This is a matter of style - you might find this gimmicky and feel uncomfortable. I have to admit it is not my cup of tea. I have, however, heard stories of clients leaning in and examining the computer screen in disbelief as they enter their targets, so I would have to suggest that if you are comfortable with that sort of methodology, you could well find it adds to the engagement process.

At all stages of the client meeting, look for opportunities to let the client discover things that they did not previously know. If you have industry benchmarking data available, use that to prompt the client's thinking. For example, an important component of any profit improvement discussion is gross profit margin. If your client's margin is, say, 62% and you are able to demonstrate that the industry benchmark is 66%, I suggest you show the benchmark to the client. But rather than entering 66% as the new target, ask the client where they would like to be relative to the benchmark. It's my experience that most clients will want to target the benchmark and some will want to surpass it. Again, although you are likely to end up with 66% in the target field, having the client suggest the number is very different from you simply typing it in.

Before a client will invest in your services to assist in a business improvement project, they need to trust you in that field of expertise. As previously mentioned, they already trust you to do their tax and accounts but if that is all you have ever done for them, you need to upgrade their trust to a new level. If they feel you are forcing unrealistic targets down their throat, they will recoil. Give them the opportunity to use numbers that they feel are both realistic and achievable and you will find the trust builds much more quickly. And once a client trusts you AND gets excited about the potential, you have a project.

It is important to realize that not every business is the same. Most businesses will fit into one of three revenue models:

- Number of customers x transaction frequency x average transaction value.
- Number of jobs quoted on x conversion rate x average job value.
- Number of clients x number of projects per client x average transaction value.

Sometimes you might come across a client who steadfastly believes his or her business does not fit into any of these models – and they might be right. I recall working with a client specialising in high value one-off construction jobs. We attempted to fit their numbers into the 'jobbing' scenario above but the real issue was capacity to take on more projects. They were only doing five or six a year and simply could not take on any more under their current structure. When you are faced with this sort of scenario, resist the temptation to fight the client and fit a square peg into a round hole. The client will never 'buy in' to the numbers if they believe you have forced them into a position they don't agree with. Simply have a quality conversation about the client's objectives and take it from there. (In this case, the owner wanted to extricate himself from the operational side of the business so we worked with him to systematize some processes, enabling him to free up 20% of time and take a vacation.)

Strengthening objectives using what-if planning

Strong objectives are good for you, but more importantly, they are good for your client. They provide clarity of purpose. They lay the foundations for the methodology required to achieve goals. They create a belief that targets can be achieved. And importantly, they imbue a willingness in the client to make a proper, value-based investment in your services and enter into a metaphorical partnership with you to realise the targeted outcomes.

Here is an example. Let's imagine you ask your client what they would like their business to look like in three years' time. You are likely to hear one or more of these outcomes as your response:

- Increased profit.
- Improved cash flow.
- Increased business valuation.
- Business no longer reliant on the owner.

There is really not much to get your teeth stuck into there. There is no 'from where to where' – hence no firm targets to shoot for. And there is no way of getting there. Where would you start in this scenario?

Compare the above with the following objectives:

- Increase profit by $200,000.
- Improve client service so that retention rate increases from 85% to 90%.
- Train sales team so that conversion rate from enquiry to new customer increases from 25% to 30%.
- Develop additional products and services to entice customers to spend with the company one more time per year on average.
- Improve pricing and up/cross selling to increase average transaction by 10% to $385.
- Implement cost savings and efficiencies to increase gross profit margin to the industry benchmark of 62%.

Now, that gives you something to really get your teeth stuck into. What you effectively have here is a roadmap to success. There are six clear objectives which, with focus and discipline on each one, will deliver the desired outcome.

So can you help the client come up with such precise objectives? Simple. Utilise what-if planning in your sales process. Take a look at Figure 5.2. All of the answers are there. And when you allow your client to discover the potential themselves as outlined in this chapter, they will present themselves to you. Your job then becomes very simple; you simply need to summarise the 'numbers meeting' in terms of the client's objectives. Given that they have selected the numbers, it is very difficult for them to argue with them.

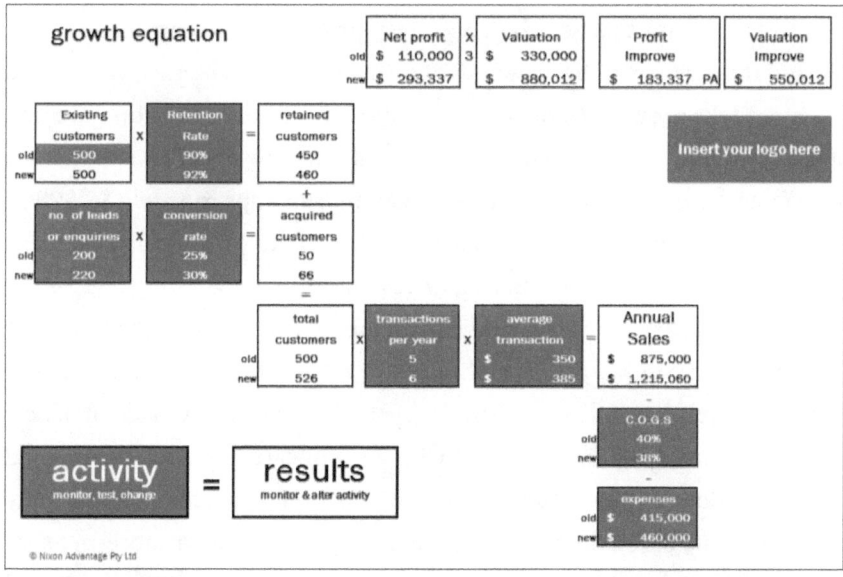

Figure 5.2 Growth equation provides clarity around client objectives for profit improvement

For clients concerned with cash flow, focus on the balance sheet or working capital drivers, being days in receivables, days in inventory and WIP and days in payables. Again, if you ask a client with cash flow difficulties what their objectives are you would most likely find that they have trouble articulating them. When cash is tight, it can become all consuming with little light at the end of the tunnel. The role you play here with what-if planning is of critical importance. With a few clicks of the mouse, you can give the client hope of a brighter future.

As you can see in Figure 5.3, by making small changes in a small number of key areas, you can often demonstrate a dramatic positive impact on cash flow. In the example in Figure 5.3, reducing days in receivables from 43 to 30 creates over $47,000 in free cash flow. Taken together with modest changes to inventory and payables, you can show the client that it is totally feasible to free up $100,000 in cash. Cash flow management is an extremely powerful weapon in your armoury. It is often said that cash is king and for small to medium-sized businesses that is most definitely the case.

I recommend that you be constantly priming the pump in this area. Become conversant in the dynamics of cash flow. You can impress and inspire clients to take action with the language you use and your conviction in using it. For example, if I have a client with $2 million in revenue, I know that for every day I can shave off receivables, I can free up approximately $5,500 in cash. It is a safe bet that no-one has ever spoken in these terms with the client before and as such you have an instant advantage.

Once final key here; use what-if planning to make the point to the client that when you work together with focus to achieve the targeted increase in the areas demonstrated by the planning, your fee is effectively paid out of new cash flow. Frankly, if that, together with a set of carefully crafted, powerful objectives does not move the client to take action, I suggest you gracefully thank the client for their time and move on to someone more open to improving their business. Certainly in my experience, I have seen more clients' eyes opened to possibilities that they had not previously considered than by any other methodology. I urge you to become familiar with it and embrace it with your clients. Until they know what is possible, they are operating in the dark. Present their possible future with passion and excitement – yet another means of building real trust with your clients in your quest to becoming a business improvement expert in their eyes.

Showing clients what is possible in their businesses

ABC & Co				
	Current	Planned	Profit change	Cash change
Balance Sheet Drivers				
Days in Receivables	43.80	30.00		47,260
Days in Inventory and WIP	19.32	10.00		21,712
Days in Payables	18.03	30.00		34,863
P&L Account Drivers				
Sales Growth %	25.00%	25.00%	0	0
Gross Profit %	32.00%	32.00%	0	0
Salaries as a % of Sales	10.40%	10.40%	0	0
Marketing/Sales as a % of Sale	6.40%	6.40%	0	0
Overheads as a % of Sales	8.00%	8.00%	0	0
Interest % of Sales	1.60%	1.60%	0	0
Taxes as a % of Profit	6.15%	6.15%	0	0

Net impact on Profit	$	-
Net impact on Cash		$ 103,836

Balance Sheet				
		Current		Planned
Cash & Equivalents				
Accounts receivable	$	150,000	$	102,740
Stock and WIP	$	45,000	$	23,288
Other current assets	$	-	$	103,836
Current Assets	$	195,000	$	229,863
Fixed Assets – Net	$	80,000	$	80,000

Figure 5.3 What-if analysis around working capital parameters can inspire clients to take action

Most clients are too close to their own glass to have clarity of vision around the opportunities in their own businesses. By embracing the power of numbers, using empowering language, implementing processes that enable clients to discover the latent potential for themselves and employing what-if planning to create a solid set of client objectives, you have an invaluable role to play in opening your clients' eyes to a brighter future.

6

The power of planning

Most people spend more time planning their vacation than they do planning their business

I strongly believe this statement to be true. We regularly dropped it into conversation with our clients during my time working in an accounting firm and there is no doubt that it resonated. If your market is small to medium-sized business, you will almost certainly find that it will resonate with your own clients as well.

Business owners fail to plan because they get too busy. They are also often focused on the wrong things, such as running a tight ship rather than investing in the appropriate resource to enable the business to grow. The upshot of this is that in many cases, the owners run out of hours in the day to hold regular Board or management meetings and it is extremely rare to find a small business with the discipline to hold an annual planning session for the year ahead.

Going back to the original statement, you would have to think that business owners do not spend much time planning their vacations either (if, indeed, they even take them)! So my conclusion is that the amount of time allocated to planning is pitiful.

It's my contention that if you are an accountant and you are reading this book, you should be offering planning sessions as the bedrock of your business improvement service. There are three reasons why I believe this:

1. It is a service that all accountants can provide. If you have the skill to crunch some numbers and facilitate a meeting, you can run a planning session.

2. Clients receive enormous value from such sessions. Over the past 15 years since leaving public practice, I have worked with hundreds of accounting firms and have strongly encouraged them to integrate planning into their service offerings. Every week I hear positive affirmations based on client feedback.

3. A planning session is the ideal platform to leverage into a range of business improvement services that can create enormous value for your clients (and for you in the process).

Let me make something very clear; I am NOT advocating that you write a 39-page business plan for your clients. Most business plans are not worth the paper they are written on and rarely see the light of day once they have been written. What I DO think you should be doing is running a planning meeting with your clients, the output of which is a concise action plan with clear accountabilities for implementation. Two very different animals. The latter is infinitely more valuable in my view.

In our business, we have adopted the One Page Plan format promoted by Verne Harnish (www.gazelles.com.) Our process has been as follows:

1. An annual planning session with all managers and directors. We work through our core values, our BHAG (big, hairy, audacious goal) and then agree upon our 10-year target. We then pare that back to 3 year, 1 year and quarterly goals and set the key priorities for the year ahead – and how we will measure the progress towards those priorities.

2. A follow-up session with the entire team where we assign individual accountabilities around projects and KPIs. All of these must feed through to the company priorities.

3. Quarterly review meetings (management followed by team) to update, revise or raise the bar on targets.

4. Weekly team meetings – entire team. Each team member gives a brief update on progress.

5. Daily management meetings – 7-minute meetings where we make commitments to each other as to what we will achieve that day. Agenda: what's up; daily metric; where are you stuck?

6. Daily ten minute meeting – all team members in the office. Same agenda as for the daily management meetings.

This process has seriously improved the way in which we manage our business. When I look back to the time we started our One Page Plan process, the number of projects we have implemented since then has been phenomenal.

Why couldn't you facilitate a similar process for your clients? I see the One Page Plan as the serious accountability model. Some clients will love it. For some very small businesses, it may be overkill. In this chapter, I will give you the process we used with our clients and which many of our Proactive Accountants Network members are using with their clients.

To pre-frame a planning service with your clients, I suggest that you go right back to the start of this chapter. Next time you are with a client whom you fancy would benefit from a planning session, ask this simple question:

'Bob, Martha, I was talking with some of my other clients recently and one of them made the comment that they spend more time planning their vacation than they do planning their business. I was wondering, does that ring any bells for you?'

And then zip it – let the client think and talk. It is a provocative question and it is designed to have the client think deeply about their approach to managing their business. Resist the temptation to jump in and fill the silence if the client does not respond immediately. As you become more involved in business improvement work, you will notice that the real value accrues when the client finds the answers for themselves.

Once your client's eyes have been opened to the fact that they (almost certainly) do not spend enough time working ON their business, they are ripe for a discussion on where they would like the business to go. Revisit Chapter 5 and specifically, be ready to encourage the client to discuss their objectives. I have found that when the client articulates a range of disparate objectives AND you have pre-framed the importance of planning, the following line works extremely well to move the client forward:

'David and Jane, you have spoken here about six clear objectives in a range of different areas. (Summarise the objectives in the client's words.) In situations like this, what our best clients decide to do is set aside some dedicated time for a planning session, which I facilitate. Is that something you would be interested in doing so that we can firm up on these objectives and put some priorities and accountability around them in the form of an action plan?'

Your clients need to be led. Few of them understand the importance and the value of planning their business and in particular, in placing accountability around specific items on an action plan. When you convey your recommended next step with confidence, you will find a good proportion agree to work with you in a planning session.

When you do engage a client in a planning session, never prejudge what the outcome might be. I once facilitated a session where the outcome was that the owners decided to sell the business immediately; in another case, it transpired that one partner was planning to retire in three years but hadn't thought to inform his partners beforehand; several resulted in us becoming involved in detailed profit improvement programs with clients; others had us establishing key performance indicator monitoring (I vividly remember a client faxing me his KPIs every single morning!); and occasionally you'll develop an action plan and the client will thank you, take it and implement it. Plus numerous other outcomes of various stripes. It doesn't matter what transpires; the key is that helping your clients to plan is a service that creates significant value.

Why process trumps content

I once worked in a small business where the General Manager was famous for his line 'my role is to facilitate.' It used to drive us crazy; in small business, there is no room on the payroll for a facilitator. All team members need to be doers with specific priorities and accountability.

But small business owners do need external perspective. And that is why an accountant offering to play the role of a facilitator in a planning session is extremely valuable. You are in and out for a reasonable fee (most accountants in Australia and New Zealand running planning sessions using our resources charge around $5,000 for the session – too cheap for the value delivered, but there you go) and because you are an 'outsider' your role truly is to facilitate – although make sure you tell it like it is, if it is clear to you that your client is going down the wrong path. That's what you are being paid to do. I know an accountant, Brett, who received the following written testimonial from a client making just this point:

> 'Brett brings external experience and expertise to our relationship and offers better advice or a better viewpoint when it comes to our own matters.'

Most accountants with whom we work would fall under the category of General Practitioner – you deal with a variety of different clients in different industries. If this is you, then you must lead with process, not content.

Consider this question from a client in, let's say, a construction company:

> 'I hear what you are saying about planning and it makes sense. But tell me, how many other builders have you done this for? What do you know about construction?'

How you answer that question is of immense importance. You can either agree with the client and run away with your tail between your legs or you get on the front foot and lead with process. Like this:

> 'I know very little about construction but that's why you should get me involved. You see, what I bring to the table is the knowledge of what works in business and what does not work. We work with over 200 business clients. Some of them are doing extremely well; others are performing not so well. We have been able to pick the eyes out of the good stuff and put together a process that we can apply across any industry.'

You might also add, depending on your level of courage, that the client presumably knows plenty about construction and yet they are underperforming. Perhaps they need some fresh eyes on the situation with someone untainted by the industry 'norms'.

This is a very valid point to raise. Sometimes we need to look outside of our own industry to find best practice. When Southwest Airlines, perhaps the world's most successful low-cost airline, was searching for how to turn planes around in 20 minutes in a quest to gain a competitive advantage, it did not go to see how American Airlines, Delta or United turned around planes. It went to the Formula 1 track.

Every time I run a planning session, I follow a simple process. It goes like this:

- **Revise profit improvement potential using accurate numbers**
  As part of engaging a client in a planning session and determining and strengthening objectives, I demonstrate the profit improvement

potential as discussed in the previous chapter. Before the planning session itself, I firm up on the numbers so that where possible, we replace estimates with more accurate numbers (remember, however, that we are aiming for success, not perfection).

- **Go through different financial scenarios**
  I prefer to discuss three scenarios which I loosely call Low Growth, Medium Growth and High Growth. Working with the client, I determine the scenario with which the client is most comfortable (needs to be both achievable and stretching) and we then lock in that scenario.

- **Discuss key points for attention relevant to the preferred scenario**
  Prior to the planning session, I have the client answer a series of questions that have them thinking about their performance in a range of different areas of their business. In the planning session, we then go through the responses and pay particular attention to those issues that need to be addressed to ensure the preferred financial scenario has the best chance of being over-achieved.

- **Develop action plan**
  Your most important tool in the planning session is a ream of flipchart paper. You will use this consistently throughout the day. When an idea comes up, capture it on the flipchart paper. By the end of the session, you should have paper plastered all around the walls. During the day, you can refer back to previous issues and remind the client what they felt was important. Out of this emerges the action plan.

This entire process is systematized for our member firms and works wonderfully well. You must consistently remember process, not content. If the client is getting hung up on technical content as it pertains to their industry, bring the discussion back to what is important: the development of an implementable financial scenario supported by an action plan with clear priorities and accountability. The role you play in keeping this on track is of immeasurable value. Left to their own devices, clients can drown in the technical reasons why 'you couldn't do that in our industry.' Your role here is to challenge and ask questions such as:

> *'Let's move into the hypothetical world just for a moment. Put aside the reasons why this is difficult to achieve. In the hypothetical world, what would you need to do to make this happen?'*

And then pick up a flipchart marker and start writing as the client comes up with ideas. Prime the pump if required with the odd idea of your own but more importantly, ask questions to elicit further ideas.

When you truly understand the fact that process trumps content, the value you provide to your client jumps through the roof. It takes practice (the hardest part can be to stop yourself talking when you think you may know the answer) but it is a skill well worth your while developing. I promise you that your clients will thank you for your independent perspective.

Why clients find planning so valuable

When I first started to run planning sessions with clients, I had a limiting belief as to the value I was creating. Essentially, it all seemed like common sense and I wasn't sure how I was going to 'wow' the client. Thankfully, there is really no need to do so (although I will write later about the importance of the little things that you make an integral part of your client service; in other words, the wow factor needs to be cultural, rather than delivered in a particular client session).

In my second client planning session, I learnt a lesson which has held me in good stead ever since. During lunchtime of a particularly tricky session (dealing with a dysfunctional family business with myriad issues that were negatively impacting business performance) the major shareholder, who happened to be the father, approached me. He had been quiet and gruff all morning. With a feeling of dread, I prepared myself for him to call on the guarantee – if you are not delighted with the planning session, simply tell us before the end of the session and we will refund your investment in full. To my surprise, I needn't have worried. He told me that if they got nothing more out of the afternoon session, they would be delighted with the value they had received just in the three hours up to lunchtime. Maintaining my composure, I found myself asking a very important question:

'Tell me, Mark, what specifically have you found valuable this morning?'

His answer was a telling one. He said that this was the first time in 12 years of running the business that the entire family had ever sat around the same table and focused on the business. As simple as that.

I quickly noticed a trend appearing in further planning sessions, where clients reported feedback such as:

- We should have done this years ago – great to spend time working on the business.
- This has been invaluable. We have never focused on the business before and tend to operate on a day-to-day basis.
- To have external input into our business has been fantastic. You should do this for all of your clients!
- Thank you for helping us come up with a plan. I am confident that with your help, we can achieve the goals we have set ourselves.

Such consistent feedback helped us understand where we were creating value. And unusually for accountants, it was nothing to do with technical expertise. Instead, it was around creating focus and discipline and providing an external perspective. That was good enough for us and it encouraged us to increase our prices. (Since our work was value priced, that was totally justifiable; we had just discovered we were way too cheap – it is rare that your clients will tell you that!)

When I left the accounting firm to start my career coaching and consulting to other accounting businesses, I ran across limiting beliefs in the minds of accounting partners when I recommended that they offer planning sessions to their clients. Beliefs such as, that wouldn't work with my clients, or that wouldn't work in my geographical location, closely followed by I don't think I have the skills or confidence to be able to pull that off.

If you have any of these (or other) limiting beliefs raising their 'yeah but' heads, let me put it to you this way. If you DON'T offer planning services to your clients, you are doing them a disservice. I passionately believe this to be the case based on consistent feedback from clients – not just my clients, but clients of many accountants. I can tell you that clients in a whole range of industries, from retail to professional services, from manufacturing to engineering, from landscape gardening to caravan parks, even farmers, value this service enormously.

Back in the mid-90s, as a young, naive consultant to the profession, and never having worked with farmers, I stupidly accepted that it might be more difficult to run a planning session with what accountants told me were 'price takers'. But I had to throw my own limiting belief out of the window, after having consulted with an accounting firm in Taranaki, New Zealand, and helped them design a planning process for farmers that they have sold over 50 times in the past 12 months at an average fee of over $4,000. Yes, it is hard to work with profit improvement potential. But by thinking outside of the box we came up with three issues of critical importance to all farmers around which we designed the service. Note the slight difference here – when operating in a niche market (in this case, dairy farmers) you can integrate content specific to that market to demonstrate your expertise. The really neat follow-up to this story is that John and Andrew from the Taranaki accounting firm then productized exactly how they work with their farming clients and have successfully sold that product via our Knowledge Factory so that other accountants with a similar client base can create massive value for their clients too.

The difficulty in a service such as planning, where the value is often intangible and hard to quantify, is the old chestnut of the first sale being to yourself. You have to believe in the value you bring to your client. You can be sure that if you do not exude confidence and talk in terms of the benefits that will accrue during and after the service, the client will smell your fear from a mile away. I hope the stories and case studies I have put forward here help allay your fears and build your own value belief so that you can put that across to the client. I admonish you to jump in with both feet to lift your own value meter – pick a friendly client, have a discussion, focus them on their lack of planning and offer a planning session. Even if you do the first one for free, or preferably, for a discounted fee so that at least the client has some investment in the process, it will be of immense value to your client and also to your own self esteem. Pick a client, set a meeting and give it a go.

CASE STUDY

I received a call from Nic, an accountant in Melbourne. Nic had sold a planning session to a client but had no idea what to do next! All credit to him for not being afraid to put himself out there. I walked Nic through the process articulated in this chapter and encouraged him to schedule the session and give it his best shot. Nic followed the process and the client was delighted.

Inspired by the glowing praise he received from his client, Nic went on to approach other clients. Within two months he had sold a further 10 Planning Sessions and eight follow-on consulting jobs including restructures, cash flow generation and profit improvement plans (including KPI monitoring). These services were all sold with an average upfront fee of $8,000-$9,000 and annual fee of approximately $15,000.

Pretty good going from a standing start but certainly not unusual when you embrace the concept of planning with your clients.

How to create a powerful action plan with guaranteed additional work for you

The key to a powerful action plan is relevance. Your client must be able to discern a clear link between the items on the action plan and the achievement of the goals and objectives that they have articulated. Short and concise beats long and waffly every day of the week.

As you consider the validity of an item proposed for your action plan, you should once again start with why. Why are we considering this particular action item? To what greater gain does its implementation contribute? To which specific objective does the action item pertain?

In our coaching work with accounting firms, we allow just three projects to be entered onto the 90-day action plan. We have found that implementation is higher and much more focused with a small number of items on the action plan. It is important that the client comes up with the action plan, rather than you – but you must challenge the projects the client proposes to run with.

Let's take ourselves back into the meeting room with the client. We are nearing the end of the planning session. There is flipchart paper all over the walls and it is time to pull everything together into a coherent plan. Here is how you do it:

1. Suggest to the client that you have covered a lot of ground and that it is now time to create an action plan for them to take away and implement so that they get maximum benefit from the session.

2. Explain that you will use the flipchart paper to summarize the day and ensure all of the important items are acted upon.

3. Move to the first flipchart paper (it is important to number your pieces of flipchart paper so that you can summarize in an orderly fashion.) Spend no more than a minute summarizing the discussion you had that led to the points noted on that piece of paper.

4. Go through each point in turn. If a point is duplicated elsewhere, cross it off. If several points can be categorized together, bracket them as one action point.

5. Move to the next piece of flipchart paper and repeat the process. Go around the room until you have discussed them all.

6. Explain to the client that an important part of the accountability process is that they select the projects that they feel are of greatest importance. Tell them that you are going to let them have 15 minutes on their own to write down the top three projects that they will commit to implementing in the next 90 days. Encourage them to think long and hard about it and to use the full 15 minutes to reflect on the session and plan for the future. Ask if they have any questions; once they are comfortable, leave the room.

7. Return in 15 minutes and ask the client to read out their number one priority for the next 90 days. Ask the following questions after they have read out the project:

    - Going back to our preferred financial scenario, which dimension of the business is this project aimed at? (For example, increasing the number of customers, increasing average transaction value, improving margins etc.)
    - Specifically WHY do you feel this project is important? (Guidance: what is the critical success factor that requires attention?)
    - Who is going to be accountable for the delivery of the project?
    - By when will it be implemented?
    - What goals will be achieved by implementing this project?

- How will you measure progress and outcomes in respect of this project?

8. At this stage, it is appropriate to provide input, recommendations and suggestions with regard to the proposed project. This might result in a wording of the project being tweaked slightly; or an extra component being built into; or the project being changed completely.

9. Repeat points 7 and 8 with the other two projects.

10. Have the client sign off as part of the accountability process.

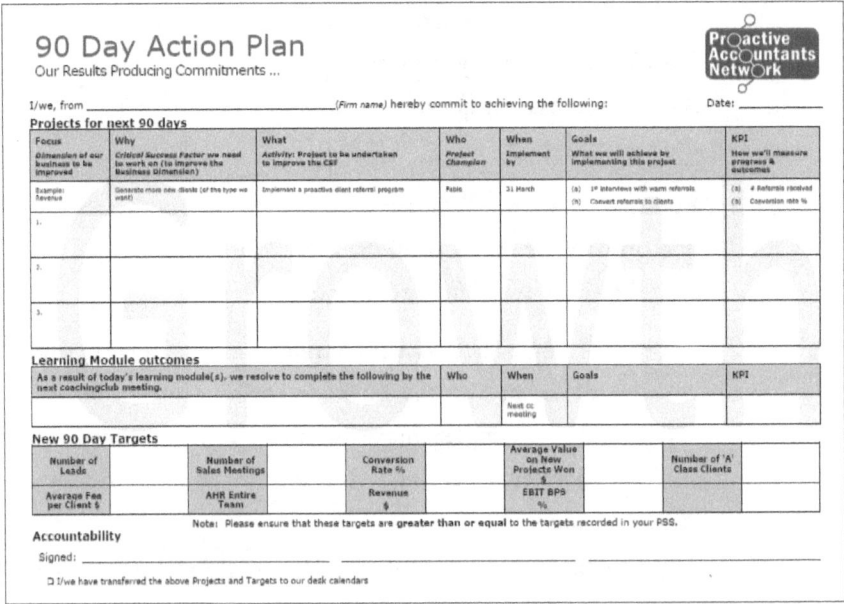

Figure 6.1 Sample 90 day action plan

By following these ten steps, your client has a powerful action plan. All that remains is to offer your help in implementing the plan. You do that by asking the client the following question:

'Denise, that is an excellent action plan that, when implemented, will move you strongly towards the objectives we discussed. If I may, let me ask you one question: do you feel confident that you can implement the action plan on your own or do you feel you would benefit from our getting involved with you in the implementation phase?'

Again, clients need to be led. They don't understand what happens next. So you need to ask this question so that they understand that you are able to be as involved as they wish you to be. In all of the planning sessions I have run, only one client has ever said in response to that question that they are confident they can implement on their own. I can only put that down to the fact that they attribute the outcome of the day to the role you have played thus far; as such, the level of trust increases dramatically and when you provide a forum for them to continue with the relationship at this higher, much more valuable level, many clients will accept the invitation.

I found that the most common 'next steps' from a planning session were in the following three areas:

1. Monthly meetings – check in, update on financials and action plan.

2. KPI monitoring – in addition to the meetings, a regular process of the client reporting back the KPIs; the more frequent the better, as it allows you to step in and recommend corrective action as and when required.

3. A full profit-improvement program where you might get involved in interviewing customers and team members, reviewing costs, facilitating workshops; a much higher and more valuable level of involvement.

In virtually every case you will create additional revenue for yourself. Even if a client says they will take the action plan and run with it, you should thank them for the opportunity to work with them in this new way and ask if it would be OK to call them in two months to see how they are going with their implementation. Once they realize they need external accountability to make things happen, they will likely request your further involvement.

Planning is extremely powerful. Ensure all of your best clients know that you can offer it as a service. And be alert for opportunities to step in and suggest a planning session. Both you and your clients will benefit enormously.

7

Monitoring and Accountability

Accountability as a major key to implementation

How many New Year's resolutions have you kept going for longer than a few weeks? Unless you are one of the few with very strong self discipline, you will be able to count them on the fingers of one hand. But why does this happen? We all have good intentions to turn over a new leaf. We feel good about the changes we are about to make...but by the end of January, we have slipped back into our old ways.

Many people have similar experiences after attending a seminar or workshop. You enjoy the event and come away laden with ideas. Then you get back to the office and suddenly you're swamped with everything you have to do on a day-to-day basis. The new ideas, which seemed so inspiring and easy to implement just a day prior, take a back seat - and very quickly slip down the priority list.

The reason? No accountability. Much as you might think you can hold yourself accountable, it is never as easy as it seems. This is the reason most diets fail. One of our most successful strategies to recruit accountants into the Proactive Accountants Network is to call them six months after they have attended one of our workshops and have a discussion around what they have implemented. Without the accountability provided by coaching, the answer is often very little. They realize they need that accountability if they are serious about changing.

From my house in Maleny in the Sunshine Coast hinterland of Queensland, Australia, I have a wonderful view of the Maleny Showgrounds. Every morning at 6am, rain, hail or shine, a group of fitness enthusiasts gather to be put through their paces by their a personal trainer who brands himself as Tribal Training. It seems to me that there is always a full complement of people. Much as I think they are crazy as I see them running up hills with a truck tyre on their back, I have to begrudgingly admire their commitment. But would they turn out without their accountability to their Tribe and its leader, Jason? I have serious doubts. (Jason's positioning is very neat, by the way. In a small, tightly knit community where everyone knows everyone, he has created not just accountability to the 'tribe' but is also extremely aware that all of his tribe members are conscious of the fact that if they drop out, the whole town will know of their 'failure' in no time at all.)

Here is another extremely contemporary example. On 23rd November 2011, my business partner, Rob Nixon and I were flying home having delivered a seminar to 90 accountants in Melbourne. Over a quiet drink on the plane, we were discussing our plans for 2012. Rob turned to me and said: 'You know, I might write another book.' I thought for a moment then said, 'Don't do that - I'll write one instead.' Quick as a flash, Rob moved into accountability mode. Within five minutes we had agreed that the book would be launched at our annual conference on Hamilton Island on 11th March 2012. Given that the publishers need two months' lead time, we determined that the manuscript would need to be delivered by 10th January. This left me seven weeks to author my first book! On 17th December I was scheduled to fly to Hawaii for two weeks' vacation which I decided I would really rather not work through. So I created a new artificial deadline for myself to have the book finished by 16th December.

Is it possible to write a book in three weeks? No sane person would think so but under the right circumstances, I have proven that it is. And I firmly believe that accountability plays a huge part in that. You see, not only did I make a commitment to Rob, but to a lot of other people as well. First thing in the morning, Rob emailed our entire team letting them know of my commitment. Next, he wrote a post on our web-based forum, subscribed to by 1500 accountants, announcing my book and its delivery date at the conference. As a result, there has been a lot of chatter on the forum and requests for me to update everyone with my progress. I have also received personal phone calls and emails from clients congratulating and encouraging me. How could I not deliver on my promise with so much accountability?

Speaking of Rob, I know many people were inspired by his running the London Marathon in 2010. Battling serious injury throughout his already short training period, it would have been easy to shelve the project for another year. But because Rob had told so many people that he was going to run the marathon, he persevered and finished the race within his targeted time and without walking (he publicized both of these goals to anyone who would listen). Several of our clients were inspired by Rob's feat to also run marathons, spurring themselves on by injecting a high level of personal accountability into the process.

I see similarly impressive achievements in business every day of the week. Accountants making difficult decisions, (e.g. terminating intractable team members, firing problem clients, removing underperforming partners) because they have made a commitment to others outside of their own partnership to do so. Specific tasks, specific deadlines and a project champion with whom ultimately the accountability rests. Just recently, I received an email from a now sole practitioner who had made a commitment to extricate himself from a very difficult partnership (difficult because he was good friends with a business partner who was seriously underperforming). He is now happier and more financially successful than at any time in his career. His email was simply to thank me and the rest of his Accountability group for keeping the pressure on with the accountability. Without it, he said, he would never have taken the tough decisions needed to set him free.

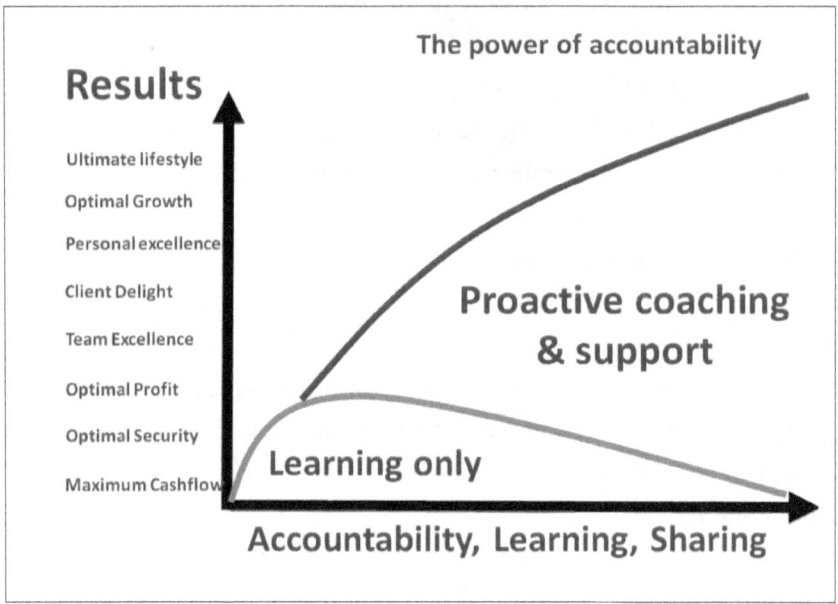

Figure 7.1 The Power of Accountability

Every day of the week, businesses and individuals around the world are planning. Setting brave new goals, charting new horizons. Plotting new ways to change the world. Yet planning and setting strategy is the easy bit. Anyone can do that (let's face it, a lot of consultants make a lot of money doing it)! The hard piece is what really counts - following through and implementing. That is where serious accountability comes into play and where you can play a game-changing role with your clients.

Stay close to the numbers

Remember my hypothesis on trust: you have instant trust and credibility in areas where you have previously worked with a client. In the case of your technical heartland of tax and accounting, you have that trust and credibility even BEFORE you do any work with this. It is assumed that you know how to balance a ledger and file a tax return.

As soon as you cross the line from technocrat to business improvement expert, your instant credibility takes a hit. Your clients may have never seen nor envisaged you playing in this space before. For some, it may be a bridge too far. For others, you need to build their trust. That is why you should stay close to the numbers.

I have encountered many accountants over the years who have forayed into business improvement, only to give up, battered and bruised, without ever making a success of it. My observation is that in most cases, their positioning was all wrong. They attempted to persuade clients that they could be marketing gurus. They spoke of reviewing websites, critiquing marketing pieces, coming up with new product ideas and taking them to market. All wonderful, noble suggestions - but can an accountant really do that? (That is the question going through your client's mind, by the way!)

By changing your positioning, you can expect a very different outcome from the client. As an accountant, your area of expertise can be loosely described as 'numbers guru.' So play in that field and leverage into new services.

One of our New Zealand based members, Geoff, found himself with a desperate client running out of cash rapidly. Geoff bravely grabbed hold of the issue and strongly recommended to the client that they needed his help as an external CFO. Although he underpriced the job hideously at $2,500 per month, by staying close to the numbers he helped the client survive and ultimately thrive, earning himself big fees going forward in the process. Had he suggested to the client that they hire him to turn around their failing marketing, I am certain his recommendation would not have been entertained.

As explained in Chapter 6, if your client has selected the right projects, they will drive the numbers in the right direction. The key to holding the client accountable is to get the client very focused on implementing the projects and then to educate them in the impact that is having on the numbers. For example:

KPI: Increase average transaction value by $50.

Related project: Create and implement a script for all sales assistants to use every time to increase cross-selling.

In your role of staying close to the numbers, in this case you would do four things:

1. Ensure the client understands exactly what the average transaction value is today (e.g. $230).
2. Ensure the client understands exactly what the target average transaction is and in what time frame (in this case, $280 in three months time).
3. Ensure that the client has selected a big, meaty project that will drive that number in the right direction; that the project has been communicated to all relevant members of the team; and that appropriate accountability has been placed around the delivery of the project.
4. Design and implement a measurement system so that both you and the client know in real time (or as close to real time as possible) whether or not the project is on track.

When explained in these terms, the client has no leap of faith to make. Everything covered in these four points lie well within your instant credibility. If the client cannot write the script themselves, by all means offer input but I suggest you consider outsourcing copywriting and other similar tasks to the experts, who will charge you a low hourly rate in return for their services.

When asking clients for case studies and testimonials, live by the same rules. Try this test; which testimonial creates more trust and credibility?

Number 1: 'We worked with ABC & Co and they did a great job to help us grow our business.'

Number 2: 'ABC & Co showed us how by increasing the average value of a sale by $50 we could double our profit. They helped us measure exactly what was happening around the key numbers and played a valuable role in holding us accountable to do the things we knew we needed to do to make it happen.'

Which one has more power and credibility? To my mind, I would take action on number 2 every time (assuming I liked the accountant and felt we could work together) whereas I can imagine many business owners being sceptical about the first one. Yet go to 10 accountants' websites and, assuming you can actually find any testimonials, I am willing to wager that 90% of them will look like number 1.

As you adopt the role of the wielder of the accountability stick, become skilled at challenging your client. The language you use is, as ever, of immense importance. Think about this in a variety of scenarios - face to face, phone or even email.

Three months ago, I received an email from one of our members, Glenn. Glenn had set his accounting firm a challenging target of $175,000 revenue for the month of August. When he set the target, he felt that anything over $150,000 would be a great result. On 30th August he sent me an email with a chart showing fees for the month to date of $152,000 against a yellow line representing the target of $175,000 with a message, 'What do you think?' My response was to the point: 'What do you need to do to get above the yellow line?' Without the accountability, Glenn might have settled for beating $150,000. Armed with my response to his email, he gathered his team around and they set about billing everything possible on the last day of the month. They reached $175,000 with an hour to go.

Instead of accepting excuses from your clients as to why they have not achieved their numbers, push back with questions like this:

- How focused were you on that target?
- When precisely did you know you were running behind the target?
- What did you do to attempt to get back on target?
- What have you learnt to ensure this does not happen again?

Use your comfort with numbers to give you the confidence to push back strongly and challenge your clients. Do not accept excuses and be prepared to tell the client that their performance is not good enough. You are there to help the client improve their business. If you accept mediocre, you can be sure your client will follow in your footsteps.

One final word of advice here; even if the client is killing their targets, be prepared to layer in even more accountability. There is nothing so guaranteed to inspire an ambitious client as the line: 'That's a great result – well done. Now, what do we have to do to raise the bar even further?'

Your role is to provoke, not to be liked

Accountants have this terrible knack of taking things personally. If one client complains on price, we think every client is unhappy. If a client we think would be perfect for a planning session turns us down, we don't ask any more because they would obviously refuse as well. And heaven forbid we should get a bad score on a feedback form at a seminar or workshop! After all, our clients are supposed to like us. Aren't they?

Well, no actually. Your clients pay you to help them. Not to have a mate. And whilst I am not saying that you should go about 'de-friending' your clients, everyone needs a bit of tough love from time to time. As the trusted advisor, it is your place to give it.

As you work with your clients in monthly or quarterly meetings, holding them accountable for the numbers and projects they committed to, you need to find some mongrel within yourself.

I'll admit that this is not the easiest thing to do, especially when you have a long standing relationship with a client. The key is to ask permission to take a contrarian stance. Like this:

> *'Tom, I am delighted that we will be working together in this new way. It's my experience that our clients get the most value out of this sort of process when we hold you well and truly accountable for the delivery of your targets and projects. From time to time, if you don't do what you say you are going to do, and when it is in your best interests, I will tell you in no uncertain terms that your performance is not good enough and challenge you to do something about it. So that we are both on the same page here, is that OK with you?'*

When explained upfront like this, you will be pleasantly surprised at the positive response you get from clients. Ambitious people acknowledge the need to be held accountable. One of the first questions I ask a new client is, 'What are you here for? Why coaching?' Nine times out of ten, accountability is cited as one of the desired outcomes. As soon as I hear that, I always make a point of rolling out the script above. I have never had a client say they do not want me to go hard on them.

As of the time of writing, we have 285 members in the Proactive Accountants Network. In our Brisbane office we have a Wall of Fame. We take a photograph of every client and ask them to write a sentence about their experience with us. My estimate is that every second one thanks us for the accountability.

Here are some tips to help you play the role of bad guy:

» **Accept only valid reasons, not excuses**

You will hear a variety of excuses as to why projects have not been completed or targets achieved. Your role is to work your way through the smokescreens that will be presented and have clients focus on the real reasons why progress has slowed. Clients will find every reason under the sun to offer up as excuses;

no time, key person has left, problems with a customer, personal issues at home, and so on and so on. The moment you accept an excuse as a valid reason, you have dug a dangerous hole. Push back immediately you smell a rat. Simply ask:

> *'Is that a genuine reason or just an excuse?'*

Clients will soon get the picture and start to drill down to the underlying reasons. It is usually simply a lack of focus and discipline – easily fixed by scheduling activities in a calendar.

» **Work with observed behaviour only**

People will blame other people to get themselves off the hook. I recall a situation working with a light engineering firm. The business was experiencing workflow problems and in two consecutive monthly meetings, the Managing Director (my client) blamed the operator of one particular machine. Apparently this operator was hopeless, lazy, did not believe the targets could be achieved and had a glass-half-empty attitude.

I was tempted to advise my client that the fish rots from the head down and challenge him to do something about it but something did not feel right. Since we were at the client's premises for that particular meeting, I asked if I could have a wander around the floor and perhaps talk to the operator in question. Upon arriving at the operator's machine, I noticed it was down. I asked the operator why that was the case and how often it was down. His reply? At least three times a day. And, he added, he had been recommending to the boss that the machine needed a major haul or replacing for 12 months.

Only ever work with observed behaviour. Ignore hearsay until it is validated.

» **Sweeping generalizations**

I learnt this lesson from an early business improvement client – a baker. We recommended he consider a price increase. The client replied that he could never increase his prices because 'I would lose all my customers.' Never accept such an outrageous response. Lose ALL your customers? Really?

I have found that an excellent question to counter this particular objection is 'what's your evidence for that?' (I borrowed that question from Alan Weiss and wholeheartedly recommend it.) Most clients will have the wind taken out of their wings and will ask what you mean. You can then point out that they are making assumptions as to what the entire market might do. In this case, the reality is that you might lose some customers, but probably only a small number. Staying close to the numbers, you can show the client exactly what proportion they could lose before they are worse off.

I see this one all the time with accountants. They take on a project – for example, pricing upfront. They approach one client who expresses concerns about the new approach. It is usually someone who has been a client since Noah built the Ark who says 'come on, we've been working together for donkey's years. You know you can trust me. Just send me a bill when you've done the work.' And they assume that ALL clients are going to have similar objections. The stark reality is that they don't.

» **Priority, not time**

The most frequent excuse I encounter is 'we didn't have time to do that.' Your response is simple:

> 'It is not a question of time; it is simply a question of the priority you chose to place on the project. When you set the project, was it important? Yes? Well why didn't you schedule the time to make it happen?'

Gimmicks can be fun and help to make a point. My partner, Rob Nixon, has been known to threaten delinquent members with *The Motivator* – a cattle prodder! Whilst *The Motivator* is live and loaded, I hasten to report that no accountants have been harmed by it (so far)! Sometimes, a bit of fun can break the ice and help our members get serious.

Figure 7.3 *The Motivator* works wonders in inspiring our members to take action!

The ultimate in proactivity - real time monitoring

Cloud accounting is all the rage. I recently attended the annual Accountants' Technology Showcase in Melbourne. There were 31 exhibitors, all vendors to the profession. Every single one of them either has a solution in the Cloud or is working towards one.

In Australia and New Zealand, the main combatants in providing Cloud accounting for the SME market are Xero and Saasu. Both of these are well-funded businesses with established client bases. Xero reports over 200,000 users in over 100 countries. This number is growing rapidly. The estimate just in Australia is that there are approximately 70,000 businesses already using Cloud accounting systems.

This, the cynics say, is just a drop in the ocean compared with the total number of businesses in Australia (estimated to be around 2 million). And yet even in these early stages, there is a 3.5% take up. In 1991, technology consultant Geoffrey Moore wrote a ground-breaking book, *Crossing the Chasm*. Moore draws on Everett Rogers' diffusion of innovations theory which shows that with any new technological advance, 2.5% of the market will jump on it immediately. They are the innovators. They are closely followed by the early adopters – a further 13.5% of the market. The early adopters and innovators want technology and performance.

Only once those two groups have taken up a new product will the majority follow suit. They want solutions and convenience (both of which are provided in spades by Cloud accounting systems) but they will not buy until other people have. There is a 'tipping point' at around 15% of the market where everyone starts buying the new technology. Moore refers to this as crossing the chasm.

Compare it to Internet banking. At first, the majority were sceptical – they were waiting for the innovators and early adopters to check it out and give the thumbs up. Now, do you know anyone who does not have Internet banking?

Monitoring and Accountability

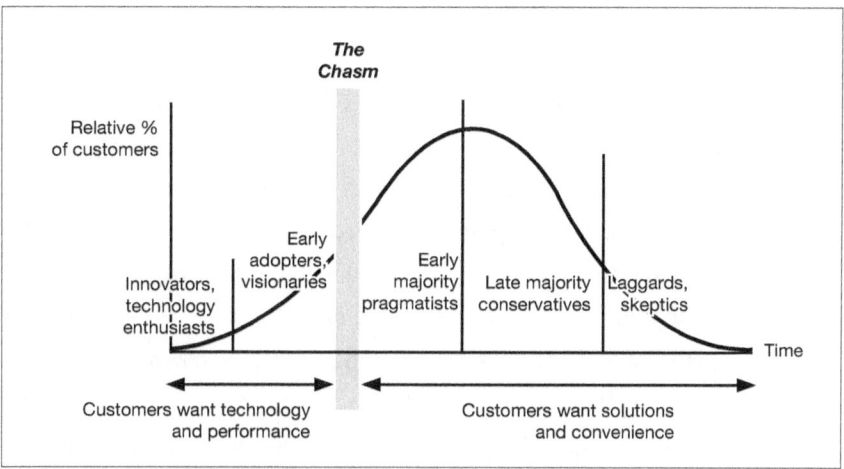

Figure 7.4 Crossing the Chasm

It's our belief that the same phenomenon will happen – very quickly – with Cloud accounting. If you share that belief, you would be well advised to take a position of leadership right now and promote Cloud very heavily to your clients.

The initial impact of Cloud accounting will be that even more efficiencies will be found, enabling accountants to do the year end work more quickly and you will have the opportunity to get closer to your client because you are both looking at the same set of numbers in real time. Very quickly – and it is happening already – there will be a secondary wave of impact. Clients will start to realise that it is taking you less time to do the work. That, combined with innovative accountants aggressively marketing a lower cost, higher-value solution to clients will put serious downward-price pressure on compliance work.

So, how to respond? I recommend you do three things:

1. Embrace Cloud accounting. Get your own firm on it. Make a commitment to migrate all of your clients to it.
2. Promote it very aggressively to your clients. Sell the benefits of going to the Cloud.
3. Move into higher value services, enabled by Cloud technology.

Imagine waking up in the morning and turning on your computer (or your iPad, for that matter). Overnight, your Cloud KPI monitoring system has received feeds from all of your clients' Cloud accounting systems and updated a dashboard summary of your clients' financial position in real time. Right there on the screen you can see that four of your clients appear to have a problem – one of the KPIs that you have agreed with them has drifted into the red zone. You instantly send an email to each client concerned, flagging the issue and advising them that your PA will be organizing a meeting to discuss what is happening and what corrective action needs to be taken.

At that meeting, you sell the benefits to the client of having a full KPI monitoring system, updated in the Cloud in real time, on their own system. It is a system that is skinned in your firm's colours and with your logo – it looks and feels like your own product. A system that enables what-if scenarios, planning for the next financial year, recording projects and ultimately real-time benchmarking for their business against other similar businesses in their industry. And they have to do nothing to keep it up to date – it all happens automatically, in the Cloud.

How much more valuable do you think you have just become in the eyes of the client?

Sound futuristic? It's not. It is all here now. Real-time monitoring, enabled by the Cloud; a system that enables you to be the ultimate in proactivity simply by REACTING to what you see on your dashboard! On any particular day, you know exactly which clients need a call, email or meeting from you and you have a specific reason for that activity. No need to sell anything – this sells itself and creates enormous value for clients in the process.

We believe this is the way of the future, but also the way of the present. You see, if 70,000 businesses are already on Cloud accounting systems, it only needs another 250,000 or so before the systems tips and the majority start to pile on board. With the amount of money and marketing the Cloud accounting providers are investing in, that could happen very, very quickly. If you don't embrace this and surf the Cloud wave, it has the potential to wipe out your core service as you currently know it. Your choice – embrace the Cloud or face a cloudy future.

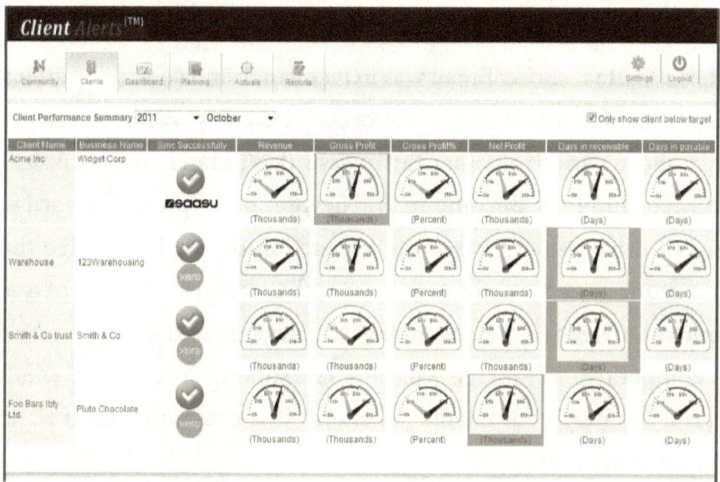

Figure 7.5 Client Alerts™ – real time view of your clients delivered by the Cloud

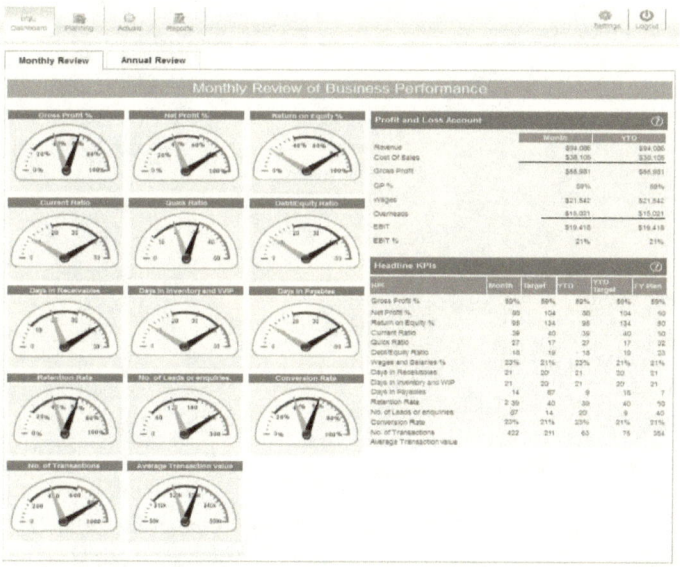

Figure 7.6 Cloud-based planning and monitoring for your clients; a very valuable new service for you

Accountants - The Natural Trusted Advisors

When I think back to the 1990s and the work we did with clients on monitoring, the labour intensity of the whole process was horrific. Only the progressive clients had computerised accounts and even they had trouble maintaining their accounts accurately. Extracting key performance indicators was often a manual chore. Email was in its infancy and so handwritten scrawl arriving on the fax machine was the order of the day. We have come a long way in a short period of time. But please don't stand there admiring the progress of technology. Become an avid devotee of it. Spread the word to your clients. Sell it hard – and base your conviction on the knowledge that real time monitoring is a breakthrough service that can give your client a serious competitive advantage. But in doing so, remember that any technology-driven competitive advantage will only last so long. You have a window of opportunity to help your clients get ahead. It is presenting itself right now. Are you up to the challenge?

8

Involving your team

Learning to let go

I too often hear the excuse that 'my team members are not capable of doing value-added work' as a reason for partners not visiting clients and undertaking sales visits (they are concerned that they will simply bring back more work that they need to do themselves). And yet many of the partners uttering this excuse have qualified accountants on their team. I refuse to believe that qualified CAs or CPAs are incapable of being involved in delivering business improvement related services (e.g. cash flows, budgets, KPI monitoring, revenue and profitability analysis, testing and measuring new ideas with a client, what-if analysis and scenario planning etc.). My evidence is based upon the fact that I have done this myself as a senior accountant and manager and I know of many others who have done the same. Here's my diagnosis. In the goal for maximum efficiency, I believe many firms have become lazy. Slash the hours to the minimum required to do the job with the necessary quality control. Here are some likely outcomes:

- Your accountants do not have time to even think about the client's business.
- They are unlikely to ask the client any probing questions to uncover unmet needs for fear of blowing the budget.
- Client service drops.
- Client needs remain unmet.
- Accountants do not develop the necessary commercial acumen to step up and become involved in higher value work, should it arise.

Please understand that this is very much a worst case scenario but I plant the seeds of it here to stimulate thought as to how you can implement simple systems to nip this scenario in the bud. To address all of the above issues, all you need to do is add two simple steps to your workflow management (only do this for those business clients where you see further potential; with the low value, churn-'em-through type client, keep doing what you are doing):

1. As previously suggested, insist upon a three-year analytical review of the client before a partner will accept the file and before the end of job meeting with the client. Those of us who trained as auditors had to do this as a matter of course. It made accountants talk to clients and get at the very least a first cut analysis of why, for example, gross margin had fallen by 3% or why sales had increased by 28%. Use technology to crunch the numbers and then have your accountants prepare some short commentary to explain them (but they must ask the client why they believe the movements have occurred).

2. Take the accountant to the end of job meeting with the client and have them observe as you take the client through the numbers and ask deeper questions. As your accountants become more accomplished and more commercially aware, based on their experience of observing you, let them run meetings with smaller clients. Chip in, help them out, but let them develop their own style.

Will all of your accountants step up when provided with this sort of opportunity? Probably not, but some will – and they are the ones whom you involve in business improvement work. But one thing we know for sure is that if you keep your accountants in the back room grinding out accounts and tax returns with no room in their time budgets to do anything beyond the bare minimum, their skills will never increase and they will either stagnate or they will move on.

My first question when I hear a partner say that they have no one on their team who could become involved in higher value jobs is 'how did *you* acquire the skills so that you could do that?' If you are anything like me, you will have been taken under the wing of a partner, someone who mentored you and got you involved in face-to-face meetings with clients. I remember my first job interview back in Chorley, Lancashire. Keith looked me in the eye and said that I would be face to face with clients very early in my career and, if I was any good, I would be doing small jobs on my own within six months. He and his fellow partners were true to their word.

To build a business that is sustainable without heavy partner involvement, you must let go. It's like monkey bars. Letting go is the only way to progress. This can be scary because you are putting your reputation in the hands of a team member. But there comes a time when you have to throw people in at the deep end.

For the first three planning sessions I was involved in, I was there to observe, take notes and chip in occasionally. Then for number four I was thrown right in at the deep end; the partner who had sold the planning session told me he had double-booked himself and I would need to run it on my own. I was the manager in charge of the client so there was a good relationship in place but I have to tell you I was terrified. Yet when we finished at 3:30pm I was elated and felt that my career had progressed rapidly to another level. Now I had the confidence to do new things, the load was taken off the partner.

Once you find a good person, throw them more and more responsibility. Of course, as the partner with the key client relationship, you should stay there in the background; a great way to do this is when you pass work over to a manager or team member, let the client know that they have ad hoc access to you whenever they need it at no charge. No client will abuse that right. It is like an insurance policy – great to know you have it in place but you don't want to be using it every day of the week.

Developing your 'A' team

By 'A' team, I mean surrounding yourself with the very best people you can get. For the purpose of this exercise, I am focusing on the team you need to make business improvement services a sizeable part of your accounting business's revenue. Set aside the people required to do the accounting and tax work, although the principals apply to any area of your firm.

Your starting point is the structure you need.

There are five functions that need to be filled:

1. Product

You need something to sell. Oftentimes in business improvement work you will find yourself going with the flow in meetings with clients and coming up with new intellectual property on the fly. That's fine, but if you want others in your firm to be on the lookout for opportunities to cross-sell clients into your business improvement service offerings, it needs to get out of your head and into a system. When we first started running planning sessions and profit improvement programs, there were only a small number of us involved in the delivery. Problem was, because we did so much of it on the fly, we were not getting cross referrals. No-one else knew what we did or how we did it. To address that, we decided to systematize our approach with clients and to give it a product name – not so much so that any accountant in the firm could deliver it (although that certainly adds value to the product) but more so that others could conceptualize the service and talk with clients and prospects about the sort of work we were able to do in the firm. Product development is an important function, although unlikely to be a full time person in most accounting firms.

With product, of course, you have a make or buy decision. There is plenty of good quality business improvement or business advisory product available for you to fast track your development. I recommend you take a good look at the various offerings and weigh up the value of buying something rather than building your own. In saying that, however, your firm should have something unique to offer the market so my view is work on a hybrid of make and buy.

Your product champion should be task driven and systems focused. You can enlist creative people to come up with product names but you need someone who can work methodically and who is good at getting projects finished.

2. Marketing
All accounting firms in growth mode should have a full-time marketing coordinator on the payroll. This is an operational role, not a strategic role. Someone to make things happen. If you are championing the business improvement service, part of your role is to come up with the marketing strategy. This might involve obtaining referrals, case studies and testimonials, nurturing bank managers, running seminars and boardroom briefings and sending out articles and newsletters. Your marketing coordinator picks up your strategy and organizes the activities required to bring it to life. The partner's role should be to turn up where and when instructed. The sole KPI for a marketing coordinator should be to maximize the number of quality leads delivered to the sales team.

I have seen a number of firms successfully outsource this role but if you are considering this, you need a very good person, especially if they are working remotely.

The natural tendency is to think that you need a super-creative person in the marketing role. Not necessarily the case. Whilst ideas are always welcome, making activities happen within deadlines and monitoring the outcomes of each activity is more important. As such, that rare mix of an analytical creator is perfect. Strong interpersonal skills are essential; your marketing coordinator will likely be dealing with venues, spheres of influence, clients and most importantly, the partners in your firm. They need to be able to communicate and also not be afraid to chase partners to deliver on promises (for example, creating case study or article outlines, or asking key clients for referrals).

3. Sales

Without sales, nothing happens. The best salesperson for introducing business improvement services to existing clients is the partner or lead client service manager. You will likely find that different partners have varying levels of skills and self confidence so consider an option whereby partners introduce one of the firm's business improvement specialists to a client. I have seen this work very well. In fact, I recall being introduced to a client by a partner in the firm as 'an expert in helping small businesses grow and one of the best people we have ever hired.' That did wonders for my self-confidence, imbued the client with similar confidence in me (we had not previously met) and also took the pressure off the introducing partner as he could then take a back seat in the sales meeting.

Once your marketing starts to deliver leads, you will find yourself in front of non-clients. Identify the best rainmakers in your firm to handle these meetings; most firms will have at least one person who stands out as regularly bringing in new work. They will be the most comfortable in this environment and as such, most likely to generate new work from meetings with prospects.

4. Delivery

You need a strong core team of people to deliver your business improvement services. You can build this up from one person initially. Involve others in your meetings to transfer skills. When provided with an environment that encourages skills development and supported by systematized products, people will step up and be willing and capable of delivering sessions with clients. I strongly believe that any good accountant can deliver business improvement work as long as they stay close to the numbers.

5. Support

A strong administrator can be an absolute godsend. Please don't get yourself into the situation where you are running around organizing projectors, screens, notepaper and orange juice five minutes before your client is due to arrive. (I can tell you from experience that this is one of the most stressful places to be!) Your headspace needs to be freed up and solid support can take a big load off. As we often tell our members, if you don't have a PA, you *are* a PA.

If you are moving into business improvement from scratch, your name may be in several boxes right now. And that's fine. But think of this as a discrete business unit and resource it appropriately as you grow. If you are a partner or other senior person in your firm, you are best suited in the sales and delivery roles. Avoid getting dragged into marketing coordination – and arm yourself with a strong PA. Once you have these five functions operating well, you have your 'A' team in place.

One final word on your 'A' team – if you have any bad eggs it can be seriously demoralizing for the quality people. In almost every firm I have ever coached, when the partners get serious about the 'A' team, they find that they have at least one person on their team who simply should not be there. Sometimes that person has been there for a long time and you can make all the excuses under the sun for not making the hard decision. But if someone needs to go, pull the trigger early. It is only fair for them, for you and for your team. When a 'cultural terrorist' is relieved of their role, you will find that even team members who have never expressed difficulties in working with that person start to come forward to thank you. You will find that the mood in your team lifts; that people are seeing opportunities, rather than problems. Barely a month goes by when I don't receive an email or phone call from an accountant thanking me for encouraging them to make a tough decision concerning a problem team member. And you know you will feel much better when you do it as well, don't you?

Investing in your people

Malcolm Gladwell, author of the seminal book *The Tipping Point*, wrote in his 2008 book, *Outliers*, about why some people succeed far more than others. He describes how acknowledged geniuses such as Bill Gates, The Beatles and many top sportsmen have three things in common:

- They had a stroke of luck.
- They grabbed the opportunity presented by that luck.
- They worked very hard to capitalize on it.

How many 'outliers' do you have in your accounting business? If you want a team of high-performing people, you need to create an environment in which they will emerge. I have certainly always considered it a major stroke of luck to join a firm about to experience a sustained period of explosive growth (our revenue grew eight-fold in the nine years I was with the firm – all organic, no acquisition). But it is only recently, and having been motivated by several partners claiming that their people are 'incapable' of stepping up to become involved in more challenging and high-value work, that I have given thought to the subsequent opportunities that were presented to me to enable me to grab hold and go along for the ride. One such opportunity, in line with the firm's policy to invest in its people, was external training.

I recall a performance review where the issue of commerciality was raised. The partner interviewing me suggested that in his opinion I needed to become more commercially aware. I offered the response that I had no idea where to start. The subsequent discussion enabled us both to discover that I was not developing in this area because I had very little confidence in entering into even basic business-related discussions with clients. Like many accountants, I was very strong technically but had had no training in more rounded business skills.

Another partner in the firm came to the rescue. He saw himself in me. He confided that when he was at a similar stage in his career, he was terrified to talk to clients and would most certainly have never considered talking in front of a group of people. He had noticed that I was reticent to contribute in meetings and felt he could help.

Involving your team

He explained that he had overcome his fears by attending The Dale Carnegie Course®. He offered to put a recommendation to the Board that the firm sponsor me to attend the same course. With trepidation, I took up the challenge. The course ran for 12 weeks, three hours a week after work. In week 13, the graduation ceremony, I found myself presenting in front of 200 people. The course had a dramatic impact on me, changed my outlook on what I was capable of doing and obtained the desired results (for me and the firm).

I am always thrilled when partners bring a young manager or senior accountant to one of our Accountability Meetings or to our annual conference. It shows me that they are committed to develop their key people. How do you expect young people to get on the same page as you if you don't involve them in the page you are getting onto?

Figure 8.1 shows the dynamics of getting the balance right between in-house, on the job training and investing in external training and education for your people. Only when you offer team members high client contact AND show them that they are important enough to warrant being sent to external courses will they become truly engaged. If you have picked the right person, they will fully buy-in to your firm's vision and be a source of new ideas that no one in-house had thought about.

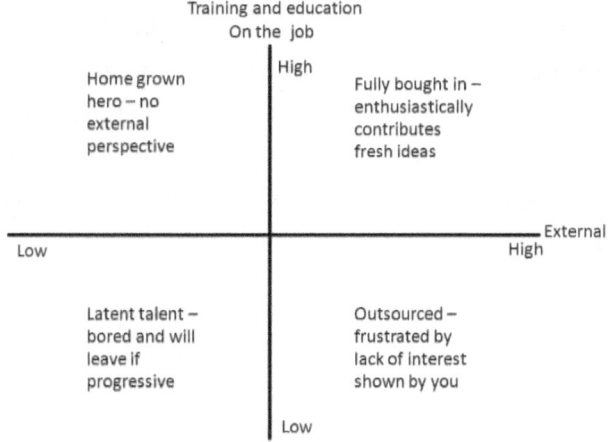

Figure 8.1 Training and education – do you have the balance right?

In our business we are constantly investing in our people. As an example, we think we run top quality events, yet we recently sent three of our marketing team to a four-day program on event management. They returned with pages of notes that will improve our already excellent events out of sight. As a guideline, we allocate 5% of each team member's salary to external education and then work with them to encourage them to spend it wisely. Another idea that we have found works wonderfully well is our book of the month. The business buys the books and provides one to each team member. They are typically contemporary business books. At one of our team meetings each month every team member debriefs on the key ideas they picked up from the book personally. One of our team collates a list of ideas and we always find something that we can implement to improve our business as well as each person individually.

On a similar pattern, we recently met with an accountant in Sydney who runs an extremely well known and profitable firm. They give a box of 12 of the best business books to every new team member joining the firm with instructions on the timeframe in which the books need to be read. The team members are then questioned about what they got out of the books as part of their performance reviews. Neat idea and easy to implement.

Here's the key; there will be high performers lurking in your firm ready to explode. But neither they nor you know who they are! So progressively offer opportunities to your team such as I have outlined in this chapter. See who steps up and give them increasing responsibility and client facing time. Encourage them through constant feedback – both praising them for specific contributions made and helping them understand how they can continue to improve. When you do that, the 'outliers' will emerge. I guarantee you'll be pleasantly surprised at the latent talent you'll uncover.

The higher your fee, the lower your involvement

Sounds counterintuitive, I know. But as you become more accomplished and have a track record of helping clients improve their business out of sight, your value increases dramatically. Equally, if you have decided to build a business within a business around your business improvement services, constantly look for ways to drive down your personal labour intensity. Your value lies in your clients having access to you when they need it, rather than you turning up on their doorstep every week.

Everything we have worked on in this chapter has been aimed at getting a capable team of people around you who can do a lot of the analysis and preparation work required to support your business improvement projects. People who can crunch numbers, help a client define key performance indicators, create systems to extract and report upon key management data, run small workshops and pull together budgets and cash flows. Partners should not be doing this work.

We have a friend, Taki Moore, who is acknowledged as the marketing guru for business coaches. Taki has a wonderful turn of phrase when assessing a potential project; he will reject it if it 'stinks of effort.' This is all about your work-life balance. As you advance in your career, you should be working fewer hours for higher returns.

So how do you do that? Well, first of all you need to accept the fact that it is not all about you. By empowering your team and systematizing your approach, you can de-you the process. I have related how I ended up facilitating my first planning session. But I was not a one-off. Within three months we had another manager doing a super job running planning sessions and team workshops with her clients. Consider the following five ideas to drive down your labour intensity and increase your profitability:

1. You don't need to be there for everything

If you have sold a project or are the lead person on the project, that does not mean you need to be involved in every single aspect of it. Introduce your excellent team members and explain that they will be primary points of contact for the client in differing areas. Pre-frame for the client right up front that they won't be seeing you every week but that you will be there, for example, for the monthly face-to-face meetings. And ensure that when you are with the client, you are really on your game, going hard with accountability and bringing ideas to the table so that your client looks forward to, for example, two hours of power with you once a month.

2. Get clients to come to you
If your clients are widely dispersed, travel can wear you down and eat into your discretionary time. Create a 'Situation Room' in your office, kitted out with the latest in technology, perhaps some inspiring artwork on the walls and an uplifting and progressive feel to the whole place. When clients visit you, ensure they are treated to a world class experience – I will expand upon this in the next chapter. When your facilities are world class and the experience the client receives at your place is memorable, they will be delighted to come to you for their regular meetings. Do all in your power to encourage this.

3. Utilize technology
If you have a remote client, consider using video conferencing for your meetings rather than either party having to drive several hours. With advances in broadband technology, products such as Skype are excellent, enabling the benefits of face to face without the hassle of travelling. We also use GoToMeeting if we need to share information on our screen with members.

4. Think leverage – one to many rather than one to one
In our business, we have developed a group coaching process that works exceedingly well, achieving far superior results for our members than any one to one coaching process any of us has ever encountered. The key is the enhanced accountability delivered by having to report in not just to your coach, but also to your peers. In Chapter 10 of this book, I will discuss how you can capitalize on niche industries – group coaching is ideal in such situations. But think also about how you might bring your clients together to help each other, rather than them becoming dependent on you. Feedback from client

advisory boards is consistent in that your clients love to be introduced. In particular, create forums, whether they be business improvement workshops or social events specifically for those clients engaged in your business improvement services. They will enjoy the experience and start to help each other. The value you provide is bringing them together.

5. Retainer arrangement
Finally, consider a retainer arrangement. View a retainer as providing the client with access to you when they need it. This is an extremely valuable service in the eyes of the client and it is often seriously undervalued by accountants when they provide it. A strict retainer involves no formal contact – the client calls you when they need you. You might also have a hybrid retainer, meaning you provide some sort of high level service and provide ad hoc access as part of that service. Some firms refer to this as a virtual CFO service. In almost all cases, I see this extremely valuable service being underpriced. I see accountants delighted at selling a virtual CFO service at $3,000-$4,000 per month. But ask yourself this question – how much would the client pay to have someone on the payroll providing the service you are offering? The answer is usually $80,000 to $100,000, with the caveat that the service would unlikely to be as good. So why are you offering it at half the price? If you sell a virtual CFO service you should price it at MORE than the market rate. Your client could not hire someone with your expertise for $100,000. Nor could they benefit from the fact that you are NOT on the payroll and, as such, if they are going down the wrong path, you would have no qualms speaking your mind and telling them. Someone on the payroll would find it hard to do that.

With a virtual CFO role like this, the value is in the access to you. Have your accounting team do the grunt work, utilizing best of breed Cloud-based technology. Minimize your appearances but aim for maximum impact when called upon.

I feel that accountants significantly underestimate how much revenue they should be able to achieve per full-time equivalent team member. The constraints are typically limiting self-beliefs based on the old model of chargeable time. In our view, a team of seven people should be able to produce revenue of $2 million and profit of $1 million (one partner, two client managers, two accountants and two administrators). But they need to be the RIGHT seven. Here is a grab bag of 20 ideas for building and keeping a great team:

1. Overhaul your website and your brand. The first thing a potential new hire will do is check you out on Google. That's your first impression. The second impression is when they turn up to your office. What do you look like? Staid, boring, same as the rest – or a cut above?

2. Your office – is it dull, dreary, a typical accountants' office? Or does it feel hip, cool and groovy?

3. Your advert – read your job ads with your prospective team members' eyes on. What have you written that will compel them to want to find out more about you?

4. Your interview process. Is it 'same same' or do you do something different from other firms? For example, how about getting multiple candidates in at once to present to you, your team and their competition?

5. Broaden your scope. Having trouble hiring accountants or grads with accounting degrees? Why not hire non-accountants (for certain services) or grads with non-relevant degrees. In 1987 I joined the graduate program of a UK firm. I was one of four grads taken on. None of us had an accounting degree. One is now a partner in that firm; another the managing partner of a different firm. Think differently.

6. Get your team involved. In your interviews; on your website; how about a brochure with little case studies and stories from team members that you give to each candidate?

7. Credo, values and service standards. What are yours? What do you stand for? How do you share these with candidates?

8. Resources – what resources do you use with clients to help them in interesting and valuable ways? Show candidates what you do, how you do it and how your clients benefit.

9. Social media – embrace it rather than banning or restricting it. At the very least, get yourself a corporate Facebook page and show it to your candidates. You want to be seen as leading edge, not in the ark.

10. LOTS of marketing – it creates new clients, which in turn create energy, a feel-good factor and new challenges and opportunities for your team. Show candidates your marketing activity calendar.

11. Seminars – do them regularly, and invite team members.

12. Value-based work – find ways to involve accountants in this work, rather than just partners delivering it.

13. Team advances – at least every six months take the whole team away to do some planning, bonding and relaxing. (You might know these as team retreats!)

14. Accountability – daily. Good people thrive in an environment of high accountability. Hold daily stand-up meetings where each person reports in on what they will achieve that day.

15. Provide exposure to clients early in the piece. When you find a good team member, get them client facing quickly. They will get bored being kept in the back room crunching numbers.

16. Let your team know the projects you have committed to, the targets you have set and the priorities for the upcoming quarter and summarize your plans for candidates.

17. Incentives – find a friend. If a team member introduces a friend or colleague who is subsequently hired, reward them.

18. Rewards and celebrations. Set challenging quarterly targets. When you achieve them, have a riotous party. Show photos of your reward celebrations to candidates.

19. Embrace learning. Our Proactive Accountants Network members have access to video-based training programs on team building. Use what you have at your disposal.

20. MOST IMPORTANTLY – to keep the right people on your team, you need to get the wrong people OFF your team. Stop procrastinating about that problem team member and pull the trigger early.

9

Building your brand through world class service

Differentiating through client service

What's more important? What you deliver, or how you deliver it? When I ran planning sessions with business clients, no client ever said to me that the agenda was well constructed, or that the day flowed very well, or that they appreciated the way we placed the financial scenario planning before the review of their questionnaire, or that the number of actions on the action plan was just right. What they said instead was that they enjoyed the **experience**, or that it was a really **valuable** day or that we made them feel **special**. 'Wow' delivery beats meticulous content every time.

I am convinced that value-based services need to be accompanied by world class service. The reason our business improvement clients felt so special was that everyone on the team adhered to our service standards consistently. The environment was extremely professional with a touch of luxury and dripping with inspiration. When clients walked into reception they were treated like VIPs.

Similarly, when accountants visit our purpose-built coaching centre for their quarterly meetings, they are treated to a special experience. Every week we receive unsolicited compliments about our team. There is always a buzz about the place that clients find uplifting.

Of course, a 'wow' environment in and of itself is not enough – you must be constantly innovating and creating value.

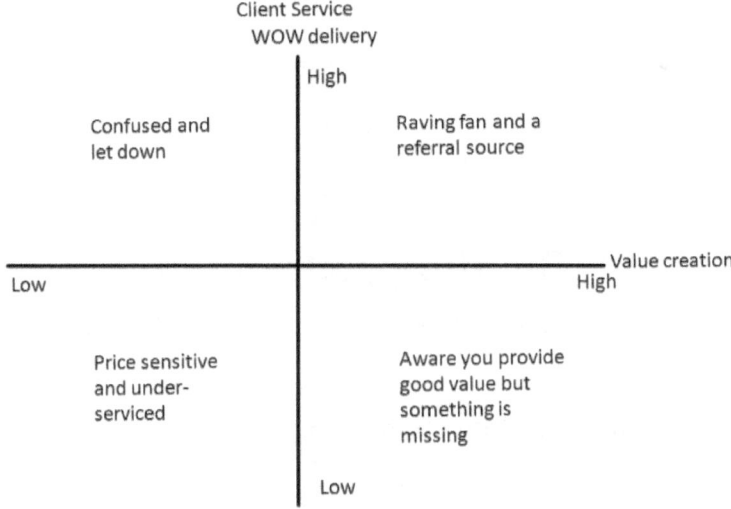

Figure 9.1 Make sure you complement your WOW service with consistently high and evolving value creation

As noted in the figure above, a client wowed by your service but who experiences little in the way of value through what you deliver, is left confused and a little let down. This would be the equivalent of a tax shop sending a limo to pick up clients to have their tax return done. Something doesn't gel.

Equally, if you create superb value for clients yet the experience they have with your service and interaction with your team is ordinary, again their perception will be that something is missing.

You need to work hard on both axes of the chart. I have spent much of this book talking about value creation so let's focus some energy on the service side of things – moving to wow.

I read a status update on Facebook recently which I loved. It read as follows:

> *If your goldfish is sick, you don't treat the fish. You treat the water. Environment is everything.*

How good is that? What are you doing to create a truly awesome and consistent environment that is highly memorable?

Here is an example:

In May 2011 I found myself transiting through Auckland on my way to a coachingclub meeting in Wellington. I came in on a very pleasant Qantas flight from Brisbane, which turned out to be the last flight piloted by Captain Larry Olsen. We were informed by Melissa, the extremely professional cabin services manager, that this was Captain Olsen's final flight in a long and distinguished career flying both military and commercial jets. This was greeted by applause from all passengers on board and then we were treated to a fire-hose farewell for the Captain by the airport fire fighters. All in all, a wonderful experience.

Just 15 minutes later, the whole thing was sullied at baggage claim. Despite being marked with a priority baggage label, my bag was one of the last to arrive on the carousel – along with all of the other priority bags. Mine looked as though it had been dragged through several hedges. A luggage tag had been ripped off and the bag had clearly been opened and not properly closed again.

This got me thinking about experiences. In our quest to create great experiences for clients, we need to be focused on making those experiences consistent. Are you creating consistently great experiences or are you consistently inconsistent?

I do worry about the slide in service standards (at least in Australia). As a case in point, earlier this year my wife and I spent a children-free weekend in Sydney, which although extremely relaxing and enjoyable, was marred by those little things that make such a huge difference. For example:

- We booked a table for lunch at Icebergs Dining Room at Bondi – a noted fine-dining establishment. The food was quality, but the service lacking. Our table was not ready when we arrived, despite having reconfirmed the booking the morning of. It took them ten minutes after seating us to take a drinks order and fifteen minutes to take a food order (too hard for the same person to do both). And we noted with some horror, several patrons dining in beach wear and even thongs (flip flops, for the benefit of non-Australian readers)!

- We stayed at the Four Seasons at the Rocks. This is one of the finest hotels in Sydney. Our request for a room to be available at early check-in was granted despite the hotel being virtually full, which had us feeling great about the hotel. However, on returning from the opera for a drink at the bar, it took 10 minutes to be served and a further 10 minutes for drinks to arrive – very frustrating, especially as the bar team were lurking at the end of the bar chatting amongst themselves.

- We enjoyed Opera Australia's version of The Merry Widow but were surprised at how few people actually dress up anymore, even at the Sydney Opera House. One man in jeans and sneakers drinking a Crown Lager out of the bottle summed it up.

Sorry for sounding snobby, but it seems to me that Australia is sinking into a morass of slapdash service and standards. And for me, at least, it leaves a bad taste.

So what can accountants do to turn that around? It's my strong belief that you are perfectly positioned to set a high standard for client service in their communities. You are in the enviable position of clients NEEDING to see you. And given that is the case, it behoves you to leave a lasting impression of the right kind. If you do that consistently and with sufficient wow factor, you will find yourself standing out as a beacon of customer service in a sea of blah. When that happens, I firmly believe you will start to attract clients of the right type.

Back in 1996 I had the pleasure of working with a true gentleman by the name of Alan Stonehouse. I had just joined Results Accountants' Systems in London and Alan was our financial controller. Alan's passion was boats and he would often shoot off to Kent for the weekend to be on the river.

Alan was an unusual financial controller in that he took an extraordinary interest in what the business did and how it helped its clients (rather than burying his nose in spreadsheets all day)! We had many discussions about the techniques we were employing to teach accountants how to help their clients run better businesses. Alan met many of the accountants we worked with and listened with great interest to the stories they told of their clients' success.

One day, he decided to follow his dream and start his own business so he bought a marina on the River Medway (http://www.cuxtonmarina.co.uk).

After I moved to Australia I lost contact with Alan for a while but recently we connected via Facebook. I was delighted to learn that his business is going strong some 14 years later. He told me that he had grown his business by focusing on three key drivers of revenue – number of customers, average transaction value and frequency of transaction. He had picked this up from the seminars we ran with accountants back in 1996.

Alan runs his business with a genuine focus on customers. In his words: "The customer's request or point of view is always right. I try to always work on the assumption that the customer's view is reasonable even if at first my reaction is the opposite. This works on several levels, we are in the leisure industry and by finding a way to meet their wishes this makes their experience as stress free as possible. You also find your stress levels are low because you know they will be happy. This "lack of stress" atmosphere is almost tangible and is a great advertisement for your business." (Notice Alan's use of the word 'experience' here. He gets it.)

Alan was fortunate. He learned critically important skills for growing a business by osmosis. Most business owners are not so fortunate because their most trusted advisor (the accountant) is REACTIVE to their needs. If you are an accountant, you need to do everything you can to PROACTIVELY help your clients achieve their goals. If you don't, you are doing them a disservice.

As you work with your clients to help them improve their businesses, customer service is an area into which you might legitimately meander. But think about it; unless your own client service is top notch, you have no right advising your clients in that area. With that in mind, let's work on a framework to help you get your own house in order.

Living by your core values and service standards

If you have the right people on your team, it is debatable whether you need to go through the tedious process of creating a set of fully documented policies and procedures so that they know what to do. A well-crafted set of core values supported by clearly defined service standards that are inculcated into your organization's culture are a very viable (and in my view, preferable) alternative.

Core values are the principles that guide your business's internal behaviour and its relationship with clients, suppliers, alliance partners and other parties that interact with you. They should be small in number (we have just six in our business).

Service standards provide the specific roadmap that dictates how your team members communicate and serve others, both inside and outside the business.

One of the best examples I have seen is embodied by the Gold Standards adhered to by every team member of the Ritz Carlton hotel group. You can read more about what they do here: http://corporate.ritzcarlton.com/en/about/goldstandards.htm. I first heard of these standards from my good friend Paul Dunn in the mid 1990s and was particularly struck by two elements in particular:
1. We are Ladies and Gentlemen serving Ladies and Gentlemen.
2. Always use the guest's name.

In 2002 I was planning a trip to Hong Kong and decided to stay at the Ritz Carlton purely on the strength of what Paul had told me - that is how powerful values and standards can be as a differentiator. We arrived on a Thursday evening, checked in and were escorted to our room. We were given a tour of the room and our view. The lady serving us even offered to unpack our bags for us. We then had a late dinner and went to bed.

In the morning we went down for breakfast. As the lift doors opened at the lobby level a smiling team member whom we had NEVER seen before welcomed us both by name! I have no idea how she did that but I am still telling people about it 10 years later. What service standards do you have in your firm that clients are telling others about?

Here is a process to help you define your own core values and service standards:

- Hold a team meeting in an inspiring location, preferably offsite. You'll need a computer, data projector, screen, whiteboard and flipchart with paper and pens

- Appoint a facilitator - consider someone external. The facilitator welcomes the participants with these key messages:

    o The purpose of today's meetings is to gather input from you in two very important areas of client service.

    o Firstly, we will be discussing something called core values. In a nutshell, these are a small number of statements that define what we stand for and what we believe in. They help us make decisions in that unless a proposed action or change is aligned with our core values, it does not make sense to do it.

    o Then, we will brainstorm our service standards. We would like to come up with a list of standards that we are prepared to share with our clients and prospective clients. These standards will provide a roadmap for people interacting with our firm so that they know what to expect when they deal with us. We would like to set the bar high in relation to service standards but equally we must be able to live by these standards every single day.

- To get the juices flowing start by going through our core values and service standards as an example (provided later in this chapter.) Whilst our business is similar to yours, it is not the same. You will get very little team buy-in if you simply copy ours. Get some feedback from the team on our values and standards. Ask for feedback on what is similar and could be used/adapted and what is not relevant and should be discarded.

- Next, get focused on your business. Start with the core values. Your optimum outcome is five or six very strong values with a short description of each. If you have a small team (six people or fewer) brainstorm this together. If you have more than six people, split the team into smaller groups (maximum group size of six). Give each team 20 minutes to discuss and come up with their suggestions for core values.

- Go around each team and whiteboard or flipchart the suggestions:
    o Eliminate all duplicates.
    o You will be left with a smallish number of suggestions. Tackle each in turn, asking for thoughts from the team as a whole as to whether the proposed value makes sense and if anyone has any objections to it. Your aim is to whittle the list down to five or six that everyone is happy with.
    o Next, turn to service standards. Go through exactly the same process as described above for core values. The desired outcome is 10-15 standards that everyone is happy with and is prepared to live by on a day-to-day basis.
    o Finally, do a sense check on the values and service standards by asking the question: "Would we be prepared to share these with our clients tomorrow?" For any negative responses, determine whether the value or standard is inappropriate (in which case, change it or eliminate it) or if it is an issue

of needing to do some work internally before you would commit to it externally (in which case, create an action plan and deadline by which you will be in a position to share it externally – use the action plan template provided).

- Next steps: publish internally, using banners, posters, intranet etc. Then publish externally – get creative with how you will do that by involving the team. As a starting point:
  - Laminate your values and service standards (double sided) as a take away for all prospects and new clients.
  - Put them on your website.
  - Put them in your newsletter.
  - Send a personalised letter to your clients launching the new values and standards.
  - Place banners in your reception area.
  - Hold an educative seminar on client service and use your new values and service standards as an example.

I hope you will have realized this is a service you can provide for your business improvement clients (but again, do yours first)!

To help you craft your own, I am including our core values and service standards. Feel free to adapt for your own use.

CORE VALUES

- **Ethical:** Doing the right things
- **Courage:** Be bold & step up
- **Caring:** Building genuine relationships
- **Open-minded:** Open to new ideas & change
- **Fun:** Do what you love & love what you do
- **Practice what we preach:** Doing what we tell

Figure 9.2 Our core values

SERVICE STANDARDS

1. I lead by example.
2. I constantly raise the bar as we lead the accounting profession.
3. Everyone I interact with will be totally delighted with what I do and how I do it.
4. I always maintain positive relationships.
5. I greet and farewell everyone by name with eye contact and with a smile.
6. If at fault, I will apologise and make restitution immediately.
7. I demonstrate a positive 'can do' attitude at all times.
8. I focus on solutions to clients' challenges.
9. I am creative and innovative in my approach to helping our clients succeed.
10. I always act with integrity and use empowering conversation.
11. I always reply to all communication by the end of the same business day that it was received.
12. If I receive a query or complaint then I 'own' it and it is addressed within the same business day that it was received.
13. I answer the phone within 2 rings & with a smile "Welcome to Proactive Accountants Network, this is [first name], [last name]."
14. I realise that I am always 'on stage'. I use the proper vocabulary with everyone I meet. I use words like 'Good Morning', 'Certainly', 'I'll be happy to' and 'My pleasure'.
15. I always live and demonstrate the company values of: Being ethical, courageous, caring, open-minded, fun and practicing what we preach.

Figure 9.3 Our service standards

Systems to make it happen every time

The most important systems in your firm are those that ensure consistently awesome client service happens every time. Consistency is of paramount importance. It can create enhanced perception of client service. Why do people go to McDonalds to buy burgers? Certainly not for the quality of the food, but because they know precisely what experience they will have every single time.

As noted however, you need to combine great service with great value. McDonalds purvey their value via a low price. As an accounting firm, your focus should not be on price but on wealth creation for your clients.

Good people can implement well-constructed systems to create wonderful experiences for clients. From the way in which you answer the phone, to your performance standards around returning phone calls or answering emails, to your standard for turning jobs around – all of these are operational essentials – right through to the surprises that you provide for your clients.

I recall a meeting with an accounting firm in Plymouth in the United Kingdom. I had previously dealt with the client at a conference organised by our firm and over the phone but had never visited their beautiful offices before. At the time I was living in London and I had a four hour train journey to get to Plymouth.

Imagine my surprise upon arriving at the station to be met by one of the team holding a card with my name on it. And then, another moment destined to last long in the memory, as I entered the firm's reception area; a young lady behind the reception desk looked up, smiled, came from behind her desk to shake my head and said 'Welcome to Mark Holt & Co, Colin. Would you like a cup of your usual Earl Grey tea?'

Remembering what I said above about never having visited the firm before, how was this possible? There is the power of systems. As I was reading the morning paper on the train, the receptionist (or perhaps, more aptly, the Director of First Impressions as she was known) was calling my PA to ask what I drank in the morning.

Very importantly, the system then dictated that my drinks preference be entered into the firm's database so that when I next visited the firm some six months later, they were able to repeat the welcome greeting with no phone call required.

It is often the little things that make the huge differences. I have seen accountants implement the following little things that have significantly lifted client service:

- Drinks menu – espresso coffees made with a real espresso machine; a fine selection of teas; top of the range sparkling water; beer, wine, even champagne. (No client will ever ask for champagne but many will comment on it. However, a client seeing you at 4:30pm after a long day might love a cold beer. Why not?)

- Food, especially at lunch time. Either a selection of snacks or offering to go out and buy a sandwich for a client.

- Parking meter top up – ask the client to leave their car keys on reception so that if their meeting over-runs, the meter can be topped up by one of the accountant's team members.

- Car valet service – once you have their keys, why not go overboard with your 'A' class clients and organise a valet service for them while they are in a meeting at your place?

- Clever database management, so that a receptionist can greet a returning client (or even a first time visitor) with 'would you like a cup of your usual Earl Grey tea?'

- Phone answering service – offer to answer the client's mobile phone and take messages whilst they are in a meeting. Not all will accept but they will remember and talk about it.

- Client photos in the database, so that receptionists (or Directors of First Impressions, as many firms call them) can recognise an expected guest and greet them by name.

- Concierge service – offer 'A' class clients 24 hour, 7 day per week access to you for anything, explaining that you can use your network of clients and contacts if they have a problem. 'A' class clients will not abuse the privilege but again, it will become a major talking point. (I heard this from an American firm. The only time it was ever used was when a client had a family member in town for Thanksgiving who needed a doctor urgently and could not contact one. He called the accountant who called a doctor client who was happy to help out.)

- Parking space reserved with the client's name on it.

- Welcome Fred and Joanne Smith – board in reception.

- Business Centre in reception – a place where clients can check email, access the web, print, access their networks.

- Have longer meetings professionally catered. Some firms I have worked with have a proper kitchen adjoined to their Board Room and bring in professional chefs to cook lunch whilst they are conducting planning session or other multi-hour meetings.

- Spend more time with your clients. Drop in unannounced. Visit them free of charge. Ask them questions about their personal interests. When you know more about someone, you can't help but treat them better when you see them.

Incidentally, I know of two firms whose Director of First Impressions have become so renowned for their service that they have been asked by clients to come out and train their team in how to provide better customer service (for a fee, of course).

In our business at a recent team meeting, we brainstormed what we could do to lift our own level of client service to another level. In just 20 minutes, the team came up with 49 ideas which we are progressively implementing. What could you do in your firm to stand out? Feel free to take any or all of the ideas above but do involve your team and add your own. Let's start a movement in client service led by accountants. Show you care and great things will happen.

No matter how good you are, there is always room for improvement. I first mooted some of the ideas in this chapter in a newsletter article and within one hour of the newsletter being sent out, I received the following email from one of our highest achieving members, Peter, in Melbourne:

> Hi Colin
> Just read your article in the newsletter. What a fantastic read and how true. Imagine what our paying clients would say to family and friends about us. I am on my way to New York but I know what I will be implementing upon my return.

Here is the litmus test; next time you walk through the front door of your office, put your client eyes on. What do they see, hear, experience, even smell? How are they greeted? Are the systems you thought were in place actually being followed? What is there for the client to read whilst they wait for their appointment? Can they see evidence of the great things you do for other businesses? Or does it just look like a typical accountants' office? Whatever you find, resolve to make it even better, then take action and put systems in place to make the experience 'wow' for your clients every single time.

Powerful feedback systems

Imagine one of your clients sitting down at a luncheon with several other business owners. The subject of accounting services comes up. What will your client say about you and your firm? Will it be positive or negative? Or worse yet, nothing at all? Will your customer stay silent, listening carefully to what's being said by others while internally running down a list of comparisons of your firm vs. other firms being discussed?

It's a given that clients are thinking about you and the service your firm provides. Even if they aren't talking about you to other business owners, they're evaluating your firm every time you provide a financial statement, tax return, or other service.

They're also evaluating your firm every time you answer a phone, return a call or send out an invoice or email.

Ironically, it's often the non-technical aspects of what you do that are noticed most. We know that clients often leave a firm not because the firm was technically incompetent, but because of the way in which they were treated.

It comes down to the issue of perceived indifference. The little things that communicate to the client that they aren't as important to the firm as they think they should be.

What are your firms' areas of perceived indifference? Your phone procedures? Your billing procedures? The way you deliver a set of financial statements? The amount of contact with your clients? The attitude of a team member? Accessibility? Timeliness?

Whatever your issues of perceived indifference, you owe it to yourself to find out what they are and fix them – now! Every day you wait, you risk losing a client who feels unheard or uncared for.

So, how do you determine your issues? We've found the best way to reveal what those issues are, is to ask. Here's the really important part: you must really listen to your clients. They already have the answers and are more than willing to share them. A great way to extract those answers from your clients is to run a Client Advisory Board (CAB).

When you think about it, wouldn't it be better to get your clients talking to you directly about their concerns, frustrations and desires, rather than telling someone else? Of course it is, but the benefits don't just stop there.

Here's the interesting part. You and your team probably already know much of what your clients' concerns are. It may be that the greatest benefit from the feedback you get at the CAB will help set your priorities as you go about implementing some of the ideas in this book.

Based on the intensity level of your client feedback, you'll know which issues need to be addressed and in what order.

Beyond that, your team will be motivated more than ever before by the feedback; you see, if you have not been through this sort of process before, for the first time, you and your team will be held accountable (there's that word again) to a whole new level of client expectation.

So what is a CAB? In a nutshell, a CAB is a small group of key clients who meet with an independent facilitator to discuss a range of topics that, in effect, will help you improve your business.

It is a forum in which you can test ideas, exchange best practice concepts and learn how your clients perceive you and your business. They know you, are familiar with your business, and, will want to help you succeed. By seeking their advice, you'll also more than likely strengthen your relationships with them.

I have run 71 CABs in my time. Only once has there been any seriously negative feedback provided by clients (a client stood up in the first five minutes to proclaim he had waited 26 years to tell the partners what he thought of them, and it wasn't good!) but even in that situation, the partners concluded that it was the most worthwhile exercise they had undertaken for many a year. Better to know than not to know and with the knowledge, they were able to rebuild and strengthen relationships with their best clients.

A well run client advisory board can provide you with input in the following areas:

- Why clients decided to appoint your firm as their accountants.

- What clients would say about you if asked for an opinion on their accountant.

- How your service stacks up against other businesses with whom the client deals.

- An assessment of how well your clients understand and use your full range of services.

- Some ideas as to additional services from which clients feel they might benefit (be careful with this one, however – as I said in an earlier chapter, clients do not know what they don't know and it is very difficult for them to conceptualise a service that does not yet exist. Innovation is your role, not your clients').

- Some specific recommendations as to how the firm could improve its communications.
- Areas where clients feel frustrated with the firm's service.
- Feedback on the office environment (this can be extremely eye opening; I remember a client of an accounting firm in the North East of England telling me that he could never concentrate on what the partner was telling him because all he could focus on were the pigeons 'crapping' on the window ledge behind him).
- Feedback on the firm's brand and image in the community.
- Ideas from successful business people (assuming you choose the CAB participants carefully) on the first thing they would do if *they* were the Managing Partner of your firm. I have heard ideas such as:
    o Develop a professional network to assist clients.
    o Provide tips and tricks for clients.
    o Take a more active stance in the community.
    o Consider a series of workshops on business growth.
    o Move offices to somewhere more convenient with car parking.
    o Undertake a serious office makeover; one client told me 'I have no idea how their team work in that office – it's a disgrace.'

One very important peripheral benefit of asking for feedback using a CAB is that clients really enjoy the process. I frequently hear clients say that this is the first time they have met other clients of the firm and they enjoy the experience. You see them swapping business cards and stumbling across new opportunities. I often ask a final question, being 'would you be prepared to do this again in six months so that we can measure progress and get your feedback on some of the things the firm has implemented as a result of your feedback?' Clients typically answer in the affirmative.

It's my strong opinion that accountants who are classified as 'rainmakers' are not great salespeople per se; in fact what they are outstanding at doing is building trusting relationships with their clients so that clients more readily take their advice when it is offered. The focus MUST be on the client at all times. Set yourself realistic timeframes and schedule sufficient activity with those clients with whom you genuinely want to work more closely to give both you and the client the opportunity to build the trust you both need. Back that up with world class service, using some of the ideas put forward in this chapter, and you will have genuinely fulfilling, longer lasting and mutually beneficial relationships with your clients and set yourself up to attract more clients just like them.

10

Expanding your Footprint into Niche Markets

Essentials for developing a niche

Once your firm is in growth mode, I see niche markets as a major opportunity to differentiate your firm and command premium prices. If you get this right, you have a real opportunity to dominate your chosen industry in your chosen market.

In my view, there are six areas on which to focus:

1. Get clear on your offering

In our business, we operate in a clearly defined niche market – we only work with accounting firms. We have learnt from past experience that one to one coaching is limited in its effectiveness, lacking the enhanced accountability of a group environment, but also the lack of leverage that one to one provides is an inhibitor to growth. Our core offering is very clear; we provide a group coaching program that gets results. We run our sessions in our purpose built coaching centre, meaning we can control the environment and the outcomes. Whilst many aspects of the content, location of delivery and people delivering have changed over the five and a half years of our flagship offering, the basic offering has remained constant from day 1: accountability, learning and sharing. What offering could you provide to your chosen industry? Could you replicate what we do? Or do you have something else that works beautifully well for you that you could expand?

2. Develop a revenue model for your niche industry

No matter what industry you are focused upon, the revenue model concept applies. What is the revenue model for your industry? Is it number of customers x transaction frequency x average transaction value? Or number of jobs quoted for x conversion rate x average job value?

Once you are certain of the revenue model for your niche, block out half a day and brainstorm strategies in each revenue-driving area, along with ways in which your target industry could become more efficient and better manage cash flow. If you know the industry well, this will be easier than you think. To help with the process, why not involve a friendly client operating in your chosen niche? You will end up with hundreds of 'what to do' ideas and your client will receive tremendous value from the session.

Once you have your revenue model documented along with your core 'what to do' ideas, you have the basis for the content you will deliver to your niche for years ahead. And it will become apparent to you as you read this chapter that being viewed as an expert is much more important when operating in a niche industry than when you are predominantly a generalist (where process is more important than content).

3. Get yourself a big database

Why not go national straight away? If you are in Australia, go to www.mailinglists.com.au and select your industry. For example, in an Accountability Meeting with a group of our members we did a quick search on pharmacies. It appears there are 3,713 pharmacies around Australia. The complete list can be had for $186. If you had a penchant for pharmacies, why wouldn't you grab that as a starting point? We have over 26,000 accountants on our database. It is a big job to keep it clean and updated but it is an absolute gold mine. There are three pre-requisites for growth; great brand, big database and loads of activity. If you don't have a database, no one is listening to your message.

I find many accountants to be ultra conservative. A typical thought process would be, it would cost me around $5,000 to do a direct mail to that list of 3,700. What if we don't get a return on that? Well, even at one half of one percent, which is the commonly expected return rate for a direct mail campaign, you would create 15 to 20 leads for your offering. If you convert just one you are ahead. If you're serious about specialising, you need to invest in a database and then market to it. Which leads to point 4:

4. Marketing

Lots of it. Build a social media presence around your chosen industry. This is free and provides you with a platform to push content to your prospective clients. My Twitter followers are now over 1100 in the ten months since I opened my account (at time of writing - please follow me on Twitter @col_nixonadv). I tweet every day; some of it is my original content, via my blog; and then I retweet content that I feel would be of interest to accountants and their clients. We have nine Twitter accounts in our business and we have started to pick up fee-paying members from Twitter at zero cost of acquisition. One of our Proactive Accountants Network members has won two new clients as a result of our LinkedIn adverts for directing business owners to www.proactiveaccountants.net.

But don't just stick to social media; traditional marketing is important as well. Ask for referrals in a systematised way. Deliver case studies via your website and in hard copy marketing materials. Run seminars, breakfast briefings, teleseminars, webinars, offer free reports or downloads. Write a book. See what works for you and then do more of that (and test changes to or cut out the activities that do not work so well). Only by generating lots of activity can you make decisions on the best approach for you to get in front of prospects.

5. Create a body of work

You need lots of content. Start a blog and use it to record your musings and observations. It will become a veritable library of useful content. Write a newsletter article on your niche industry at least once a month. Create a seminar series and run it monthly. (Test what works best for your niche industry – breakfast briefings or late afternoon tend to be the most attractive but it will differ by industry.) If you're not comfortable in front of a group, get some help in that area.

Revisit your revenue model from step 1 above and start to create content that you could deliver to clients around this model. Create an annual benchmark report and open it up to non-clients as a value add and a prospecting tool. We put out a benchmark report on the accounting industry every year. The 2011 report attracted over 50,000 downloads. Every single one is putting up their hand as at least showing some sort of interest in what we do.

One big red flag to be aware of, however: you do not need to create all of your content before you launch. I know people who have spent millions on product or content development but nobody knows about it because they have not invested enough time or money in taking it to market. Get your offering out there and then create your content as you go.

6. Become the go-to person for your chosen industry

If you are specialising, you need to be an expert. This is a very different position to take from being a generalist. As an expert, you need to know everything about what makes the industry tick. Just as we know everything about what makes a successful accounting firm, you need the answers for your niche industry. Put yourself out there as a leading expert and support that claim with position papers and thought leadership. Get close to press contacts who write on behalf of the industry that interests you (you will find them in industry magazines and on websites and blogs). Offer to provide them with content at no charge (e.g. a monthly article on best practice in the industry). Let them know that if they are looking for a comment on a development in the industry, you would welcome their call. And perhaps most importantly, get off the fence and be controversial. You need to move people to want to work with you. By being controversial and speaking your mind, you will polarise people. Some will dislike what you say – don't worry about that. Just get ready to work with those whose interest you pique and put their hands up to participate in your valuable program.

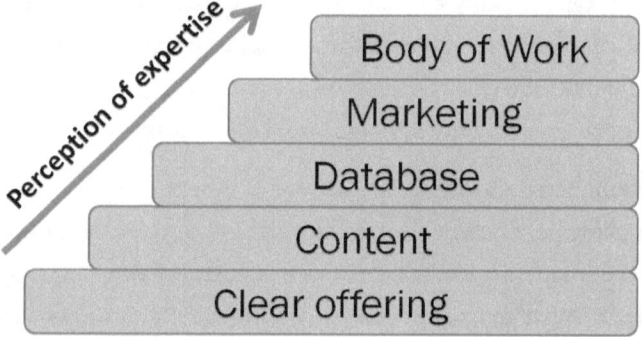

Figure 10.1 The more you do and the more consistently you do it, the more you will be perceived as an expert and become the go to person in your chosen industry

Becoming a content expert

One of the questions I am most frequently asked is where do I get all my content from. I find that one of the excuses accountants use to avoid writing is that they do not have any content or any ideas as to what they might write about.

Perhaps counter-intuitively, if you have this challenge I suggest you start a blog. I use my blog to capture ideas but also to impose accountability on myself to write regularly. My performance standard is to blog at least once a week. By blogging regularly you create a catalogue of really neat content that you can leverage in the future. Whether you blog or not, you need a mechanism for ensuring your great ideas do not disappear into the ether.

So once you have a mechanism for storing your ideas, the only question is, where do you get the content from?

I recall a very productive session in an Accountability Meeting with eight proactive accounting firms. We allocated part of the day to reviewing real life examples of financial statements for business clients. I split the group into teams of four and gave the teams half an hour to come up with as many ideas as they could to take to the client to improve their business. All of the groups filled at least one sheet of flip chart paper. In one case, the potential value to the client was generally considered to be so high that it would justify an investment of over $100,000 over three years to implement all of the ideas. This was a $5,000 client.

During the session, I noted down two 'killer' ideas to share via my blog:

1. Demonstrate to the business owner how much (or little) they are making per hour worked in the business. In this case, given what the accountant knew of his client, the calculation came out at $18.60 per hour. What an eye opener that would be for a business owner – and what motivation to improve the business's performance!

2. One of the accountants slipped this into the discussion: "How about going to the client and discussing 10 strategies to increase profitability?" Sounds simple? Many of the best ideas are. The key to simple ideas like this is how you leverage them. As a team, we then came up with 10 ways to leverage this idea (in two minutes flat):

    i) Brainstorm 10 generic ideas with your team and use them as the basis for a profit improvement program (either one to one or one to several with clients).

ii) Create a coaching offering around your ideas.

iii) Conduct a brainstorming meeting with the client and prioritise the top 10 (this could be a charged service or a free, marketing service).

iv) Write a booklet "ABC & Co's top 10 ideas to improve the profit of businesses in Your Town" – sell the booklet.

v) Make the booklet available as a free download on your website in exchange for contact details of prospective clients.

vi) Condense the booklet into a flyer and use in your new client pack or marketing collateral.

vii) Create a seminar around your top 10 ideas.

viii) Gather 10 case studies from real examples of how you have helped a client in each area and use them collectively and individually in your marketing.

ix) Support your case studies with testimonials.

x) Use all of your ideas as the basis of internal training programs to upskill your accountants.

Similarly, I recently facilitated a session where eight accounting firms each presented a case study of great work they had done with a client. Throughout the session I kept detailed notes, asked questions and provided feedback. The title of my notes? Blog ideas. Three blogs eventuated from that session alone. And some of those ideas have found their way into this book.

In my book, client case studies and articles should be a cornerstone of any marketing collateral you produce. I admonish all of the accountants with whom I work to write on a regular basis. A major contributor to building trust with clients is to demonstrate credibility. If they can see you have 'done it before' with a real person or company, you are in a great place when positioning a new service to help the client.

Yet too often I am told 'I can't write' or 'I didn't have the time to do that article.' Come on. It is not difficult. It is simply a matter of priorities.

Earlier this year I was proud as punch to be able to watch my now 8 year old son, Matthew, being presented with an Excellence in Writing award at school. A poem he wrote is to be published. If Matthew can be excellent at writing, so can you.

All of this reminds me of something I wrote as an addendum to an article last December. I am reproducing the addendum here to support my view that it should take you 45 minutes to write an article, not 45 days.

How to write an article in 5 easy steps

Here are the five steps I use to write an article every month – you should be doing the same as part of your marketing strategy:

1. Capture topics during the month. I write an article a month. I usually capture four or five themes and use two or three of them as the basis of my article.
2. Have someone remind you to write the article. In the middle of every month our marketing coordinator sends me a reminder of the deadline for submission for the newsletter.
3. Schedule in time. When I receive the reminder email I immediately schedule a suitable time to write the article. In this case, a three-hour plane journey from Brisbane to Auckland – great use of time.
4. Scratch out an outline. In the Qantas lounge at Brisbane at 4:15am I spent 10 minutes doing my outline with a latte in hand.
5. Write the article. Discipline yourself to write during the time you have set aside. Don't be tempted to go back and make it perfect. Remember – success, not perfection!

I tell people it should take 45 minutes to write an article. I spent 10 minutes on my outline, 28 minutes on my article leaving seven minutes for this bonus for you!

What is your technique for creating content to add value to your clients and demonstrate how you can best help them achieve their goals?

There are ideas everywhere – but how many ideas like this go through to the keeper? Get into the habit of writing down your ideas then actioning them. You'll find your firm, your team and your clients will be improved as a result. The good news is that creating content for a niche market is easier than being generic. Your content creation **process** is the key. Then get totally focused on the content you create in the knowledge that it will be relevant to every single potential client in your target market.

One final note on content creation (and it is an important one) is you do not need your entire suite of content before you launch to your niche market. If you think about it, all you need is some initial marketing content to get you going. You can create your delivery content as you go. In our business, we are six years into working with accountants and we are constantly creating new content. It is never finished, so please don't try to finish it before you get cracking!

Developing and qualifying your prospect list
Now that you have a list of potential prospects and some initial content and positioning material to get you started, it is time to begin the process of qualifying your prospects and converting them to clients. I am often asked whether the list should be large and unqualified or small yet prequalified. I favour the former approach. Let your potential prospects determine whether or not they want to work with you, rather than the other way around.

Let me give you an example from our business, which given we are talking about offering business improvement services to a niche market – in our case, accountants – is a perfect role model for you to follow.

This year, we acquired a dead cold list of 55,000 tax agents, available in the public domain. The available data was simply the name of the agent, their business name and street address. In some cases we did not even have the name of the agent – just business name and street address. How on Earth do you warm up a list like that?

Well, the approach you need to take is multifaceted. No one activity is likely to convert people from a list like that into a client overnight. You will also no doubt be thinking that a direct mail campaign to a dead cold list could be somewhat risky; in this case, sending one piece of mail to them all could be a $150,000 operation.

The key is to test your approach. Our marketing team decided to run a test with 1,000 names. They started from the beginning of the list and used the first 1,000 names – note again, do not attempt to pre-judge, let the market determine their level of interest. We hired a copywriter to create a nine page letter promoting my business partner Rob's book to the 1,000. Some of the letters were addressed to 'Dear Managing Partner,' so cold was the list.

We were astonished by the response. From the first test of 1,000, we had a 5% response rate of people buying the book. The key is that this approach offered a low cost entree to experiencing our firm – we are talking about a $30 purchase. So, 50 firms buy the book. Are they now clients, or even prospects? No. We call them participants. They have chosen to participate in some sort of experience that gives them some sort of feel around our content. The profit on the book sales did not cover the cost of the marketing campaign but we figured that one new client would cover it, so worth a test.

We had a small number of people proactively contact us as a result of reading the book, seeking further information. As a result of one of those, one of our sales team spent 40 minutes on the phone with someone who had put their hand up and implied 'I now declare myself a prospect' and made a sale. Excellent outcome.

All 50 book buyers were asked to provide their details (including name and email address) in exchange for giving them the right to purchase the book and all willingly provided that information. Now we are getting somewhere. Once an accountant provides us with their email address, they are automatically added to our electronic newsletter list. Every edition (there have been almost 70 at time of writing – once a month on the first of the month) provides some value in the way of content relevant to an accounting firm – usually a main article, some tips and tricks, perhaps a client case study – and then there is always a subtle sell or call to action at the end. We receive enquiries from the newsletter every single month. And, of course, all recipients have the right and ability to unsubscribe instantly should they wish to.

Two weeks after the dispatch of the book, one of our sales team calls the new prospect to ensure the book arrived safely, see if the prospect has read it and ask what they found particularly relevant to their firm. A good proportion of those calls turn into full initial consultations, enabling both parties to determine whether we are right for each other.

Those who do not become a member straight away go into our warming up process. We do this by pushing out regular content to all contacts subscribed to our list. This is predominantly email based content, whether it be the monthly newsletter, industry specific white papers, industry benchmark reports or invitations to webinars or face-to-face events. The key is to offer a variety of different ways in which prospects can experience what you do. Our marketing rhythm with our list of prospects is three pieces of value followed by one sales piece.

The benchmark report in particular is a great interest generator. We are able to capture real time data on the accounting industry using our Cloud-based monitoring system, enabling us to create a comprehensive benchmark report quickly and efficiently. Having your finger on the pulse of the industry numbers goes a long way to giving you massive credibility. If you are interested in getting really serious about doing the same in a niche that interests you, we are currently building a similar system for general business that we will be able to adapt and license for different industries. This will give you a huge leg up to dominate your chosen niche. Once again, it is the process that is the key; adapt your content to a proven process.

As another example, our members use a web-based lead generation tool called TRUST to determine where clients have needs and develop a prioritized action plan. The tool is totally customizable, meaning that if there are specific questions or issues that are pertinent to your chosen industry, all you need do is adapt those questions or issues (your content) to the proven process (TRUST) and you have a custom built tool for your niche. Such a tool can help enormously in developing prospects into clients.

As you become serious about developing a market niche, managing and developing your database becomes a critically important job. We have one person full time on our database. She plays an integral role in delivering leads to our sales team. All firms in any sort of growth mode should have a full-time marketing coordinator on the payroll. If you are serious, make sure you have all the appropriate resources.

Making it happen with a marketing activity plan
When contemplating marketing, a common mistake is to spend too much time on marketing strategy, branding and positioning and not enough time on lead generation. Marketing consultants are very good at spending your money on spiffy new websites or a brand overhaul and frankly, most firms starting on this journey do need this. But be aware of this key point; the person or firm that does your brand makeover might not be (in fact, quite likely is not) the person who kick starts your lead generation. Marketing professionals tend to specialise. Some are great at advertising. Others have a creative bent and can create wonderful branding that positions you superbly. Of late, a new breed of social media consultant has emerged. But make no mistake, once you have your rebrand done and you have a good looking website, almost 100% of your marketing effort and spend should be allocated to lead generation.

As I mentioned in Chapter 8 (Involving your team) the marketing co-ordinator role can be quite analytical by nature. So you want someone who is good at implementing projects; who can take an idea and create activities around the idea and make them happen; can organise for the partners to turn up on time and in the right place with an audience to speak with. You need a marketing **activity** plan, not a strategic marketing plan.

Note the wording well. A major key to marketing is to schedule activity and make it happen. New clients and new work of the type you want rarely just walk through the door. We see a positive correlation between those firms who engage in lots of activity and those who create the most new business. One logically follows the other.

Whether you are marketing to an industry niche or to business in general, there are three keys to an effective Marketing Activity Plan:

1. Schedule marketing activities every single month.

2. Allocate somebody (preferably a marketing coordinator) to make the activities happen from an administrative perspective so that the partners, directors and other senior team members involved in business improvement can simply turn up as scheduled.

3. Put some accountability around the plan to ensure those senior people do actually do what they said they were going to do.

Figure 10.2 provides a template marketing activity worksheet. I suggest you organise a meeting to discuss what you are going to do to generate leads, both from existing clients and for new clients, in the next 12 months. Brainstorm ideas and record them in the Notes column.

Target Market:		
Activity	**Notes**	**By when**
Articles and position papers		
Radio interviews		
Advertising		
Listing in trade journals		
Speaking		
Website		
Newsletters		
Third party endorsements		
Referrals		
Teaching		
Products		
Networking		

Figure 10.2 Marketing activity worksheet

Do you need to plan activities in every area covered by the worksheet? No, you don't – but pick six or seven that appeal to you and add others that you and your team come up with that you feel would be appropriate. The 'By When' column is important – set some deadline and commit to making something happen.

Once you've settled on your activities, have your marketing coordinator plan them out in the form of a marketing activity calendar. You will find an example at Figure 10.3

what is our marketing plan?

what	why	who	July		August		September	
Marketing Activity	Objective		Plan	Actual	Plan	Actual	Plan	Actual
Client visits - nurturing	Offer more services to clients	Clients	20		20		20	
Searching database for opportunities	Offer more services to clients	Clients	Yes		Yes		Yes	
Newsletter (email or mail)	Build credibility with case studies	Clients/Prospects/Suspects			Yes			
Seminars	Offer more services to clients	Clients/Prospects/Suspects					Yes	
Email or mail out	Direct promotion, sell 1 thing at a time	Clients/Prospects/Suspects	Yes					
Referrals	Ask for more clients	Clients/Prospects/Suspects	Every A class client		Every A class client		Every A class client	
Cross selling	Direct promotion, sell 1 thing at a time	Clients/Prospects/Suspects	Every client		Every client		Every client	
Networking	Attract new clients	Clients/Prospects/Suspects	Yes					
Spheres of influence	Attract new clients/offer more services to existing	Clients/Prospects/Suspects	Lunch / Coffee		Lunch / Coffee		Lunch / Coffee	
Niche marketing	Attract new clients/offer more services to existing	Clients/Prospects/Suspects						
TV/print advertisements	Attract new clients/offer more services to existing	Clients/Prospects/Suspects						

Figure 10.3 Marketing activity calendar

If you were hoping to see some sort of convoluted process and your observation is that the activity calendar above is very simple, that's precisely the point. It is supposed to be simple. The key is to take away all of the barriers and excuses that prevent marketing from occurring.

Again, something should be scheduled every single month. You might, for example, commit to monthly client nurturing, quarterly seminars, bi-monthly newsletters, quarterly events for spheres of influence and a major push on referrals in, for example, August. Whatever you select, make it happen and measure the success of each campaign so that you know what to stop doing and what to continue doing more of.

Finally, ensure that you put some internal accountability around the plan. Your marketing coordinator does need to be a strong person who is not afraid of standing up to a delinquent partner who has failed to provide case study content. You might also consider this idea, implemented with great effect by our members, Brian and Kurt, partners in a growing firm in New South Wales, Australia – each morning at 7:30am, irrespective of where they are or what they are doing, Brian and Kurt hop on a conference call or convene a meeting for just two minutes to ask each other specifically what they plan to do to develop new business that day and establish whether or not they did what they said they were going to do the previously day. Because both Brian and Kurt are deadly serious about helping their clients and growing their firm, their rate of implementation is extremely high and this added layer of accountability has helped them ramp it up another notch. Great idea – take it and use it.

Final Word

Accountants consistently devalue how hard they worked to be Chartered Accountants or Certified Public Accountants or the hard-earned experience they have. I see this not only in how accountants charge for services but how they position themselves. Positioning is critical and can't be under-estimated. You must think about your dress, the words you use, the look of your office and all of the intangibles a prospect or client takes from an interaction with your firm.

How do you respond when someone asks 'what do you do?' Most accountants of whom I have asked this question respond, not surprisingly, with 'I'm an accountant.' How do you think this insipid reply might go with a stranger you meet at a cocktail party? Sadly, you might see a potential new client disappearing into the distance offering vague apologies and promising to catch up later on! I know the stereotypical image of the accountant is unfair – after all, I AM an accountant and I work with accountants every day and love doing so – but let's accept it and change our language accordingly.

To craft a better response, I suggest you sell your competency and your credentials, in that order. So instead of 'I'm an accountant,' how about 'I help business owners grow their business, increase their profit, improve their cash flow and ultimately put in place a succession plan or sell their businesses.' Such a response is much more likely to provoke a reply such as 'that sounds interesting – how do you do that?' And so, of course, you need to have a clearly articulated response to such a question. Never utter a statement or ask a question without first thinking through the various different ways in which the client might answer – and then having a response to each of them. A great way to do this, by the way, is to use case studies. Ask the prospect to tell you a little bit about their business so that you can make your answer more valuable to them. Then, once you have some information from them, talk about some work you have done with a client and the results accruing to that client in a way that you now know the prospect will relate to.

This approach is so unusual (in that almost everybody else WILL say 'I'm an accountant') that it will automatically differentiate you as someone bringing value that the prospect could use. At that time, wheel in your credentials. 'By the way, we are accountants and tax advisors too so we take care of all of that for our clients as well.' And suddenly, you have new positioning on being an accountant, whilst leading with your business improvement services.

Another way to focus others on your competencies and credentials is to develop a personal brand. Imagine if you were known in your community by some sort of brand name such as The Profit Driver or The Queen/King of Cash. Or if your firm were renowned for its Six Steps to Business Success. If you go down this line, associate your (or your firm's) name to the brand. So, for example, Albert and Bracken's Six Steps to Business Success is a more powerful brand than simply Six Steps to Business Success. Raise awareness of your brand by writing articles and white papers and making them available to all businesses in your area. Become known for something special, rather than simply being just another accountant.

Thank you for getting involved and reading this book. I trust you have found it to be of value. Now, implementation is the key. That is up to you (although, of course, we would love to help you should you wish to supercharge your implementation process).

I wish you every success in establishing yourself and your firm as a business improvement specialist. Whatever you do, have lots of fun and create enormous value for your clients in the process.

www.ingramcontent.com/pod-product-compliance
Lightning Source LLC
Chambersburg PA
CBHW021843220426

43663CB00005B/381